Neodarwinism in Organization and Management

New Horizons in Management Sciences

Edited by Lukasz Sulkowski

Vol. 1

PETER LANG
Frankfurt am Main · Berlin · Bern · Bruxelles · New York · Oxford · Warszawa · Wien

Lukasz Sulkowski

Neodarwinism in Organization and Management

PETER LANG
Internationaler Verlag der Wissenschaften

Bibliographic Information published by the Deutsche Nationalbibliothek
The Deutsche Nationalbibliothek lists this publication in the Deutsche Nationalbibliografie; detailed bibliographic data is available in the internet at http://dnb.d-nb.de.

This publication was financially supported
by the University of Management,
Spolczena Akademia Nauk.

Cover Design:
© Olaf Gloeckler, Atelier Platen, Friedberg

ISSN 2194-153X
ISBN 978-3-631-63750-0

www.peterlang.de

Contents

Introduction

> Critical, pragmatic and normative disciplines remain clearly dependent on other disciplines. For to justify their assessment and normative opinions, to build projects that can be realised and meet specific needs, they need the help of other sciences.
>
> *Tadeusz Kotarbiński*

This book was written as a result of interest in the application of the theory of evolution in the social sciences, especially in management studies. The history of Darwinism in social studies is almost as old as the history of the theory of evolution. From the historical point of view, however, 19th-century attempts at using Darwinism to examine the human mind were unsuccessful, both scientifically and culturally. Social Darwinism by H. Spencer created the potential for eugenics, which subsequently turned into the ideology of genocide in the first half of the 20th century. It is therefore not surprising that the use of Darwinism for the examination of social life was abandoned after World War II. Associating the social world with the theory of evolution lost its scientific reflection and became politically incorrect. It was not until the development of evolutionary psychology, neuroscience, primatology and paleoanthropology using brain examination methods that Darwinism returned to the social sciences.

The development of the evolutionary thought and cognitivic turn at the end of the 20th century provided new perspectives for the social sciences. Thanks to the combination of research on human behaviour in social and humanistic disciplines with neo-evolutionary theories and modern methods of mind examination, studies in the social sciences may become significantly more dynamic[1]. An important cognitive condition that facilitates the development of this interdisciplinary alliance is the transfer of the evolutionary paradigm to the social sciences. Psychology has observed a rapid development of the approach, which is referred to as evolutionary psychology[2]. Much greater are the controversies related to the application of evolutionism in sociology and cultural anthropology[3]. From the management point of view, the undertaking of analyses

---

1 C. Elworthy, *Homo Biologicus. An Evolutionary Model for the Human Sciences,* Duncker & Humblot, Berlin, Internet 1993, accessed 2007.

2 J. Tooby, L. Cosmides, 'Toward Mapping the Evolved Functional Organization of Mind and Brain' in: *The New Cognitive Neuroscience,* M. Gazzaniga (ed.), MIT Press, Cambridge Mass. 2000, pp. 1167-1178.

3 cf. E.O. Wilson, *Sociobiology: The New Synthesis*, Harvard University Press, 2000.

of the possibilities for the application of the evolutionary paradigm in our sciences seems intentional and valuable.

Here, neoevolutionism is a point of reference for the social sciences. It is possible to indicate other cognitive fundaments, such as neopositivist philosophy or hermeneutics and phenomenology, at the opposite end of the continuum. In my book, however, I have focused not on the philosophical bases of the social sciences, but on the opportunity to enrich their cognitive perspectives. The enrichment would consist in the use of the verified general theory (of evolution) and methodology derived from the natural sciences in the interpretation of social life. This brings a promise of a greater diagnostic and prognostic power for the social sciences, especially of management, and in the future, should lead to the formation of more precise theories with a more mathematised and falsifiable character. The methodology of controlled observation and social experiment enables the creation of links between social and cultural processes and the functioning of the human mind.

Simultaneously, I am not an orthodox representative of neoevolutionism in the social sciences. I am of the opinion that one should also appreciate the value of existing and previous research methods, like also other cognitive results in the social sciences. It is worthwhile, however, try to integrate paradigms with methods, which will lead to the synthesis of the natural and social sciences in research on culture, society and human conciousness.

This book also raises the topic of the use of the neoevolutionary perspective in the social sciences, especially in management studies. Sociology, anthropology and psychology are disciplines of science that emerged from philosophy in the 19th century and which focus on the cognition of the nature of man, society and culture. The Darwinist perspective, although often considered controversial, has left its mark on these sciences over the last one hundred-plus years.

It is different in the case of the management, organization and business sciences, which are younger and lack as pronounced an academic identity as the above-mentioned social disciplines. Management mainly uses metaphorical references to evolution that are related to the competition, market and life cycle of economic entities, but which do not raise the topic of analysis using the neoevolutionary perspective as paradigm. It seems that using this paradigm in the management sciences discourse could bring significant cognitive results. This is supported by several arguments.

Firstly, valuable, albeit controversial, is the application of evolutionism in psychology, anthropology, sociology and even economics. Secondly, neoevolutionism has a verified general theory and middle range theories that serve to explain many key aspects of human social life. Thirdly, the methodology of neoevolutionism is based on controlled experiments and observations that use also techniques of neuroscience and cognitivism; it is therefore a novelty in relation to the traditional methods of the social sciences. Fourthly, many matters in the management sciences deal with problems directly related to the individual and social behaviour of man, whose description is based on neoevolutionism. Decision-making, exercising power and leadership, organisation of collective action and people management, organisational communication and creation of organisational cultures are just selected examples of human actions, in the explanation of which the neoevolutionary paradigm might prove useful.

A critical look at the application of the neoevolutionary paradigm in the management sciences initially shows its inadequacy on the subject of interest of organisations and management. From the point of view of biological evolution, economic entities, markets and sectors are not the units of research and scientific scrutiny. However, a more profound analysis leads to the conclusion that the basis of the functioning of all market components is human behaviour, which can be described from the evolutionary point of view. The management sciences should accept challenges that stem from the development of the neoevolutionary paradigm and related sciences, such as psychology, evolutionary anthropology and sociobiology, because all actions related to organisation and management are marked by biological evolution.

The aim of this book is to outline the neoevolutionary paradigm emerging in the social sciences and indicate possibilities for its application in the management sciences. This monograph has an interdisciplinary nature and refers to a theory that has been formed on the basis of various social and natural disciplines, including management, psychology, sociology, anthropology, biology, epistemology and cognitivism. The work is targeted at researchers who specialise in management and other social sciences, and for whom the neoevolutionary paradigm can be a valuable point of reference.

The book consists of thirteen chapters. The first five are of a more general character, which presents the bases of the neoevolutionary paradigm in the social sciences, including management, whereas the following eight point to the application of the neo-Darwinist approach in an organisation.

The first chapter is an attempt to outline the bases of the neoevolutionary paradigm in the social sciences. Cognitive premises of the new perspective derive mainly from evolutionary psychology, which is based on the new, 20th century synthesis of evolutionary biology. The new epistemological perspective has been confronted with paradigms rooted in the social sciences, such as functionalism and interpretivism.

The second chapter outlines the perspective of the new field of research, i.e. evolutionary management, by describing the directions of development of the neo-Darwinist reflection in the disciplines of other social sciences. The analyses of the application of neoevolutionism have involved psychology, economics, sociology and anthropology. Experiments using evolutionary thinking in these disciplines might serve as sources of knowledge, theories and methods for the management sciences.

The third chapter analyses possibilities for the application of the neoevolutionary theory in the management sciences. The conclusions show that neoevolutionism has opened the sciences to new horizons, which will enable reinterpretation of many organisational and management phenomena from the perspective of the description of human social nature that is rooted in the process of evolution.

Chapter four describes possibilities for the application of the methodology derived from neoevolutionism in the examination of problems in a social group and organisation. It indicates possibilities for the use of innovative methods of controlled observation and experiment in relation to the social sciences.

Chapter five, which deals with primatological inspirations in management, describes possibilities for drawing conclusions on the development of human cognitive and social skills, including organisational skills, in comparison to primates. These analyses, based on many years of observation and experiments, have revealed that at the core of organisation there is also instinct, which humanity has inherited from their simian ancestors.

Chapters six and seven focus on the outline of possibilities for the analysis of culture in the neoevolutionary paradigm. Culture is a subject of much research in the neo-Darwinist school, from paleoanthropology, through primatology, to mathematics. Probably not all approaches will prove creative, but it is obvious that the marriage of the natural and humanistic sciences has begun to bring positive epistemological results. From the point of view of the management sciences, an important research problem is the possibility of using neoevolutionary thinking in the search for the origin, essence and typology of organisational cultures.

Chapter eight illustrates an analogy between the culture of a primitive human community and modern organisational cultures.

Chapters nine and ten focus on power, hierarchy and leadership. The chapter deals with the evolutionary conditions of power, hierarchy and aggression, violence and war. It also looks at the relationships between the processes of power and the sense of justice and the social institution of property. The chapter searches for the evolutionary conditions for leadership, which is one of the foundations of management processes. Chapter ten is an attempt to use the achievements of neo-Darwinism in a search for the bases of strategic thinking processes. Although it is generally believed that perspective thinking and planning are attributable solely to the human species, a growing amount of research results indicate the beginnings of perspective thinking in predecessors of Homo sapiens.

Chapter eleven focuses on the meaning of "common good" for the evolutionary perspective. Using the model of the "tragedy of the commons", one can describe the chances and dangers in the management of public good and non-commercial organisations, which is a key problem of public management theories.

Chapter twelve outlines the possibilities for the use of the results of evolutionary psychology, primatology and neurosciences in marketing. In addition to enriching the theory with an explanation of the evolutionary sources of heuristics and characteristics of perception, and human cognitive and emotive structure, neo-Darwinism offers the opportunity to use research on the functioning of the human mind in certain situations. Knowledge in the field of neuromarketing might be valuable from the market point of view, but its acquisition should be regulated by restrictive legal and ethical rules.

The last chapter describes the possibilities for the application of neoevolutionism in human resource management. Behavioural economy discoveries related to human cognitive illusions should be applicable to the theory and practice of human resource management. The personal sphere, similarly to most other problems in the management sciences, is based on man's social skills and organisational behaviours, which have their source in the evolution of anthropoids and hominids. The book ends with conclusions that describe perspectives in the development of, and greatest challenges to, the neoevolutionary paradigm in the management sciences[4].

---

4 Ł. Sułkowski, *Ewolucjonizm w zarządzaniu. Menedżerowie Darwina*, PWE, 2010.

Chapter 1

Neoevolutionism as the new paradigm of the social sciences

Introduction

The neoevolutionary paradigm in the social sciences is in the initial stage of development, although the idea of social Darwinism having been discredited[5], this is actually its second beginning. It seems however, that neo-Darwinism, closely related to evolutionary psychology, has in the last few decades achieved significant scientific successes, which make it more respected by philosophers of knowledge[6]. The use of neoevolutionism in research on man, culture and society involves a radical change of perspective in the social sciences and leads to man being dethroned by science once again[7]. The history of science indicates that humanity must have gradually rid itself of the conviction of its central role in the universe. The milestones of the emancipation of thought were: the Copernican Revolution, Darwinism and quantum mechanics. Copernicus put an end to the theory that the Earth was the centre of the universe. Darwin and his successors destroyed the image of man as the crown of all living creatures. 20th century physicists described a fundament of reality that proved unimaginable for man and was based on a coincidence. The time has thus come for another scientific revolution. Neoevolutionism forces its way into the social sciences and leads the challenge to the traditional vision of the subjectivity of man in favour of a hybrid called "the gene vehicle"[8].

The chapter analyses relations between the quickly-developing neoevolutionary paradigm and other paradigms of the social sciences. The basis for the analysis is the suggestion by G.. Burell and G.. Morgan to divide the social sciences into four paradigms.

A thesis can be proposed that the opposition: the standard model of the social sciences versus neoevolutionism, suggested by J. Tooby, L. Cosmides and S. Pinker and accepted by most neoevolutionists, is too much of an ideological

---

5 A. Espina, 'El darwinismo social: de Spencer a Bagehot', *Reis*, no. 110, 2005, Internet edition, pp. 175-187.

6 M. Mameli, 'Evolution and psychology in philosophical perspective', in: R.I.M. Dunbar, L. Barrett, *Evolutionary Psychology,* Oxford University Press, New York, 2007.

7 D.M. Buss, *Evolutionary Psychology. The New Science of the Mind,* Pearson, Boston, 2008, pp. 36-70.

8 R. Dawkins, *The Selfish Gene,* Oxford University Press, Oxford, 1976.

simplification. In fact, although it proposes a radical change of cognitive perspective in the social sciences, neoevolutionism remains in a more complex relationship with other paradigms of the social sciences[9].

New scientific revolution

In the most popular publication on the philosophy of science in the 20th century, T. Kuhn describes the historical model of the change of paradigms in the natural sciences[10]. This has opened a broad debate on the possibilities for the application of the revolutionary science development scheme in the social sciences[11]. According to many researchers, the current stage of development in the social and humanistic sciences does not indicate the emergence of one paradigm; on the contrary, it proves the permanent multi-paradigmaticality of the social sciences. Psychology, sociology, cultural anthropology, economics, linguistics, management, business and organizational sciences, law and the humanistic sciences use many different discourses that are based on various theories, assumptions and terminology. 20th century social sciences have also seen many new interdisciplinary concepts. Psychoanalysis, phenomenology and hermeneutics are examples of theories with their own epistemological programmes and ambitions to describe the nature of man and society. None of these concepts have, however, led to a great synthesis or dominated the research perspective of the social sciences. Will this also be the fate of neoevolutionism?

Standard model of the social sciences

According to S. Pinker, the development of evolutionary psychology lead to a decline of the standard model of the social sciences, which dominated the 20th century thinking of man and society[12]. It is now being replaced with the neo-Darwinist synthesis, which offers a coherent and complete explanation of human behaviours based on reliable empirical research. Thanks to the use of scientific

---

9 E.O. Wilson, *Sociobiology: The New Synthesis* 1975, Harvard University Press; R. Dawkins, *The Selfish Gene,* op. cit.; W.D. Hamilton, 'The Genetical Evolution of Social Behaviour', *Journal of Theoretical Biology,* no. 7, 1964, pp. 1-52; R.L. Trivers, 'The Evolution of Reciprocal Altruism', *Quarterly Review of Biology*, no. 46, 1971, pp. 35-57.

10 T.S. Kuhn, *The Structure of Scientific Revolutions. Chicago*: University of Chicago Press, 1962.

11 P. Feyerabend, *Against Method: Outline of an Anarchistic Theory of Knowledge*, 1975, (First edition in M. Radner & S. Winokur, eds., *Analyses of Theories and Methods of Physics and Psychology*, Minneapolis: University of Minnesota Press, 1970.

12 S. Pinker, *Tabula rasa, Spory o naturę ludzką,* GWP, Gdańsk, 2005.

methods developed by the natural sciences, complemented with some of the traditional methods that are considered bound to the social sciences, it is possible to describe the nature of man and society, and predict and model the changes. It seems, however, that S. Pinker sees his opponent in the form of this "standard model of the social sciences". In fact, the social sciences have never seen a consensus or a dominant trend in basic cognitive assumptions, research subjects, insight or methodology.

Moreover, in the 20th century, an important role was played by the neopositivist (logical empirism) orientation in the social sciences, which used an approach that was characteristic of the natural sciences[13]. In my opinion, "the standard model of the social sciences" is one of many trends of reflection in the social sciences, which is not at all of a "dominant" or "standard" character. It is not difficult to give examples of social disciplines and theories that were not compatible with such a model, and with elements of the neoevolutionary paradigm. Looking closely at the development of linguistics, it is difficult to negate the role of N. Chomsky and his nativist concept of language in generative grammar[14]. In sociology, the development of the functionalist and neopositivist trend was also very important, which also used the theory of evolution[15]. Therefore, neoevolutionism in the social sciences is not developing in complete opposition to previous theories and schools.

While describing the standard model of the social sciences, one can point out a range of categories by S. Pinker, J. Tooby and L. Cosmides[16] that constitute its profile. Epistemological dualism involves a diversification of assumptions and methods in experiencing the world of nature and the world of man. Nature is dealt with by the sciences such as physics, chemistry and biology, whereas the human mind, culture and society – by the social and humanistic sciences, such as psychology, sociology, cultural anthropology, political science, economics, management and history. In the social sciences, cognition is based on understanding and interpretation; it is of an individual character. At the same time, it is possible to understand reality in mathematical rules and models. An inter-subjective, or even subjectivist approach indicates fundamental restrictions on the perception of the social world and the lack of

13 G. Morgan, *Beyond Method. Strategies for Social Research,* Sage Publications, London, 1983, p. 20.

14 N. Chomsky, *Topics in the Theory of Generative Grammar*, 1966.

15 cf. T. Parsons, *Societies: Evolutionary and Comparative Perspectives,* Prentice-Hall, New Jersey, 1966.

16 S. Pinker, *Tabula rasa,* op. cit.; J. Tooby, L. Cosmides, 'Toward Mapping the Evolved Functional Organization of Mind and Brain', in: M. Gazzaniga (ed.), *The New Cognitive Neuroscience,* MIT Press, Cambridge Mass., 2000, pp. 1167-1178.

possibilities for theory falsification, which often stem from cultural or epistemological relativism. Culturalism is a conviction that, mentally, the human mind is almost entirely shaped in the process of socialisation[17].

According to S. Pinker, neoevolutionism is characterised by assumptions that are contrary to the standard model of the social sciences. In epistemological monism, the mental world can be described by means of such categories of the physical world as information and calculations with the use of methods from the natural sciences[18]. In objectivism, which is the main postulate of both neopositivism and neoevolutionism, the social world is recognisable through science. Verificationism and falsificationism involve practising science through seeking to confirm or reject scientific theories (falsificationism by C. Popper)[19]. Epistemological universalism (anti-relativism) is a belief in the possibility of reaching general and unquestionable rules of science based on the correspondence theory of truth. In cultural universalism, surface cultural diversification hides deep, universal mental mechanisms that constitute "human nature"[20]. In comparison, according to evolutionary cognitivism, human cognitive skills find their place in the brain, whose development results from the coupling of genes and the environment, and were created in the process of biological evolution[21].

Table 1. The standard model of the social sciences versus neoevolutionism

Criterion	The standard model of the social sciences	Neoevolutionism
The nature of reality and cognition	Dualism	Monism
Characteristics of cognition	Subjectivism and inter-subjectivism	Objectivism
Epistemological assumptions	Interpretivism or constructivism	Verificationism or falsificationism
Influence of the context of cognition and culture	Cultural or cognitive relativism	Epistemological and cultural universalism
Subject's cognition of reality	Essentialism	Evolutionary cognitivism

17 S. Pinker, *Tabula rasa,* op. cit., pp. 32-52.

18 ibid., p. 55.

19 K. Popper, *The Logic of Scientific Discovery*, 1934 (as *Logik der Forschung*, English translation 1959)

20 S. Pinker, *Tabula rasa,* op. cit., p. 63.

21 ibid., pp. 66-70.

Research methodology	Understanding, hermeneutics, phenomenology (search for meaning)	Cause-effect explanation, experimental method (search for explanation)

Source: Own work.

Neoevolutionary paradigm

The theory of evolution is based on the concept of natural selection and functions as a paradigm of the biological sciences, which has a growing use in the social sciences[22]. Natural and sexual selection of behaviours assumes that in the long-term perspective of their existence, Homo sapiens have developed structures and behaviours that are conducive to genetic reproduction and ontogenetic survival of an individual of the species, whereas non-functional structures and behaviours have gradually disappeared[23]. The egoism of genes is based on the assumption that an individual's source of action is genetic reproduction and distribution of one's own genes, which is possible through offspring but also through helping kin reproduction, based on a common genetic element[24]. Kin mechanisms of development result directly from the assumption of the egoism of genes, and explain the question of parental care and investment, and kin altruism. Non-kin reciprocal altruism is a functional effect, which assumes that cooperation and commitments made by individuals in a group, in the long term are conducive to their individual chances of survival and reproduction[25].

Neoevolutionism has characteristics of a paradigm, as it proposes a coherent epistemology and methodology based on a theory that is highly verified and is used in many disciplines of science. However, in biology, the neoevolutionary theory is a dominant and verified concept that is based on a great number of scientific proofs; whereas in the social sciences neoevolutionism is one of many concepts for research on the human mind, culture and society, alongside functionalism, critical theory or interpretivism. Neoevolutionism in the social sciences has collected a certain amount of evidence confirming the validity of its epistemological and methodological assumptions. This was possible thanks to, on the one hand, the work of such researchers as W.D. Hamilton, R.L. Trivers,

22 J. Barkow (ed.), *Missing the Revolution. Darwinism for Social Scientists,* Oxford University Press, Oxford, 2006.

23 cf. L. Barrett, R. Dunbar, J. Lycett, *Human Evolutionary Psychology,* Palgrave Macmillan, New York, 2002, pp. 22-44.

24 R. Dawkins, *The Selfish Gene,* op. cit.

25 R.L. Trivers, *The Evolution of Reciprocal Altruism,* op. cit.

E.O. Wilson, S. Pinker, and J. Tooby and L. Cosmides, and on the other, to the fast development of mind examination techniques and the experimental social sciences. The research covers mainly human behaviours interpreted in the categories of the evolutionary developed mind, which makes it possible to predict and interpret behaviours related to social cooperation, sexual choices, parenthood, many aspects of perception and cognition, and differences between the sexes[26]. Apart from achievements in empirical research, neoevolutionism in the social sciences uses a theory that applies to the whole world of living organisms (neo-Darwinism).

According to M. Bradie, neoevolutionism in the social sciences realises two separate epistemological programmes[27]. One examines the evolution of human cognitive mechanisms, and the other – the evolution of scientific theories. The evolution of cognitive mechanisms is an issue largely under empirical research that analyses the functioning of the brain. The evolution of scientific theories is an epistemological and philosophical issue in which the theory of evolution is a source of analogies and metaphors rather than cause-effect explanations. Evolution, understood in such an indirect way, has been a source of inspiration in many social sciences[28]. For example, in economics and the management sciences, one can also differentiate two trends of evolutionary reflection. Behavioural economics deals with human economic behaviours, which are based on the evolutionary shaped cognitive system[29], whereas evolutionary economics uses analogies of evolutionary development and mechanisms of the biological section for market analyses[30].

---

26 L. Barrett, R. Dunbar, J. Lycett, *Human Evolutionary Psychology*, op. cit.

27 M. Bradie, 'Naturalism and Evolutionary Epistemologies', in: I. Niiniluoto, M. Sintonen, J. Woleński, *Handbook of epistemology*, Kluwer Academic Publisher, Dordrecht, 2004.

28 K.N. Laland, *Niche construction, Human Behavioral Ecology and Evolutionary Psychology*, in: R.I.M. Dunbar, L. Barrett, *Evolutionary Psychology*, Oxford University Press, New York, 2007.

29 A. Tversky, D. Kahneman, 'Availability: A Heuristics for Judging Frequency and Probability', in: *Judgment Under Uncertainty: Heuristics and Biases*, D. Kahneman, P. Slovic, A. Tversky (eds.), Cambridge University Press, New York, 1982.

30 K. Dopfer, *Evolutionary Economics. Program and Scope*, Kluwer Academic Publishers, Boston, 2001.

Paradigms in the social sciences

The classification of paradigms in the social sciences can be derived from the system proposed by G. Morgan and G. Burrell[31] (Table 2). The latter describes a paradigm as a socially rooted network of basic assumptions regarding the ontology and epistemology of management (the picture of reality, cognitive ideal, fundamental social value orientations)[32], which is perceived by the community of researchers in an implicit or explicit way.

Table 2. Paradigms in the social sciences

Epistemological assumptions regarding scientific ideal		Preferred social value orientation	
		Regulation	Radical change
	Objectivism	Functionalism	Radical structuralism
	Subjectivism	Symbolic-interpretive paradigm	Postmodernism

Source: On the basis of G. Burrell, G. Morgan, *Sociological Paradigms and Organizational Analysis,* Heinemann, London, 1979.

The first paradigm is called functionalist, sometimes – neopositivist or the quantitative paradigm. Its cognitive model is the natural sciences. The paradigm combines the influence of the philosophy of logical empiricism with the functionalism of sociology and cultural anthropology. The Vienna Circle heritage includes: the assumptions of verificationism and accumulation of knowledge, the search for a scientific method, the classification of dependent and independent variables, the search for mathematical modelling, and quantificational methodology[33].

In the management sciences, functionalism is a dominant orientation. Most theories aim at the realisation of the neopositivist scientific ideal. Knowledge should be objective and universal. Trends most deeply rooted in this perspective are those directly related to economics, which are also related to the birth of the management sciences[34]. Connections to economics are most visible in attempts to

31 G. Burrell, G. Morgan, *Sociological Paradigms and Organizational Analysis,* Heinemann, London, 1979.

32 cf. G. Morgan, *Beyond Method. Strategies for Social Research,* Sage Publications, London, 1983, p. 21.

33 cf. Ł. Sułkowski, *Epistemologia w naukach o zarządzaniu,* op. cit.

34 cf. L. Martan, *Rozważania o nauce o kierowaniu organizacjami,* Organizacja i Kiero-

direct management development onto a path of practical discipline of business studies. The social systems and functional vision of organisation is accompanied by the image of a resourceful man, close to the categories of Homo oeconomicus. The quantitative methodology plays an important role in such areas of management as managerial accounting, logistics and information management.

The symbolic-interpretive paradigm was created in opposition to functionalism. Its most crucial sources of inspiration are the social and humanistic sciences, such as humanistic sociology, psychology, literature studies and cultural anthropology. An attempt to reconstruct the assumptions of the symbolic-interpretive paradigm in management leads to several points, including social constructivism, the cognitive role of language in the social reality and the relationship between cognitive activity and practice. These epistemological assumptions are realised in research programmes based on the qualitative, "soft" methodology, which derives mainly from the humanistic sciences.

In the management sciences, many concepts related to organisational culture, human resource management, management and change management processes are based on the epistemological assumptions of the interpretive approach. Examples are the "sensemaking" and "loose coupling" concepts by K. Weick, the idea of organisational culture by L. Smircich or organizational identity by M.J. Hatch [35]. The basis of interpretive epistemology is the assumption on the constructivist and conventional character of the social and organisational reality[36]. Organisational order does not exist objectively but is continuously maintained, reconstructed and modified by individuals and groups, working in and around the organisation. Organisation and management processes are created by groups in the processes of institutionalisation and internalisation, and are of a contractual character, i.e. based on a collective consensus [37]. Economic matters act on a par with political, social and psychological influences. A man within an organisation searches for meaning; she or he is value-oriented and involved in a research situation. The act of cognition is entangled in language, culturally relativised and symbolic. Research

---

wanie, no. 2 (108), 2002.

35 K. Weick, *The Social Psychology of Organising,* Addison-Wesley, Reading Mass, 1979; L. Smircich, *Organisations as Shared Meaning,* Organisation Symbolism, 1983, JAI Press, Greenwich, pp. 55-65; M.J. Hatch, M.S. Schultz, *Organizational Identity: A Reader*, Oxford : Oxford University Press 2004.

36 M.J. Hatch, *Organization Theory: Modern, Symbolic-Interpretive and Postmodern Perspectives* . Oxford : Oxford University Press, 1997, pp. 24, 56.

37 P.L. Berger, T. Luckmann, *The Social Construction of Reality: A Treatise in the Sociology of Knowledge*, Doubleday, Garden City, 1966.

results are not objective, but only inter-subjectively communicable. One can notice that the focus is on the categories of everyday life that cover a hermeneutic circle in the form of perception, interpretation, definition, verification of usability and action[38].

The radical structuralism paradigm is based on the assumption of the existence of an objective social reality, which is in need of fundamental reconstruction. Social truths are hidden in omnipresent micro- and macrostructures of power. The role of the social sciences is to discover hidden mechanisms of power, domination and social inequality, and to make changes to social awareness and reality. The radical structuralism paradigm is critical of the social status quo and the achievements of the social sciences. The role of a researcher is to acquaint himself with social mechanisms and, most of all, to change the social reality. The research methodology is of a qualitative nature and is based on commitment. The radical structuralism paradigm is also referred to as a critical trend in the social studies (critical studies) and is closely related to neo-Marxism.

The fundament of modern neo-Marxism is the Frankfurt School, represented by T.W. Adorno, M. Horkheimer, J. Habermas and H. Marcuse[39]. An important theoretician who described objectively interpreted mechanisms of inequality was P. Bourdieu, who used the term "symbolic violence"[40]. In our times, S. Hall and S. Deetz continue this thinking in their critical approach towards the media and social communication[41]. Another path is neo-Marxist feminism, which describes the situation of women as a group culturally dominated by false awareness, identity manipulation and symbolic violence[42]. Social neo-Marxism has been reborn as political criticism of modern democracy, the imperialism of the developed countries and the processes of globalisation.

The trend of radical structuralism penetrates to the management sciences through the criticism of managerialism as a tool for domination and the ideology of power[43]. This is related both to feminism and the criticism of the

38 Ł. Sułkowski, *Interpretative Approach in Management Sciences*, "Argumenta Oeconomica", nr 2, 2009, p.127-151.

39 M. Horkheimer, T.W. Adorno, *Dialectic of Enlightenment*, 1947.

40 P. Bourdieu, 'Animaadversiones in Mertonem', in: R.K. Merton*: Consensus and Controversy,* J. Clark, C. Modgil, S. Modgil (eds.), The Falmer Press, London-New York, 1990.

41 S. Deetz, *Transforming Communication, Transforming Business: Building Responsive and Responsible Workplaces,* Cresskill, Hapton, 1995.

42 A. Oakley, *Experiments in Knowing. Gender and Method in the Social Sciences,* The New Press, New York, 2000.

43 N. Harding, *The Social Construction of Management,* Routledge, London, 2003, p. 14.

organisational power hierarchy, the media and social communication. For example, the management sciences, sociology, cultural anthropology and ethics literature includes anti-marketing publications, which raise the issue of the criticism of marketing as being both a science and a social practice of a manipulative and exploitative nature [44]. Some of the analyses indicate development paths for ethical marketing, based on the subjective treatment of customers and research participants[45].

Postmodernism is the least homogenous approach. It is so incoherent that, actually, it is pointless to call it a paradigm. Common elements are subjectivism, cognitive relativism, programme incoherence and distrust of science. Postmodernists question the possibility of reaching an objective truth[46]. The postmodernist trend indicates the fall of the meta-narrative of the Enlightenment project (the fall of the myth of progress), based on an uncritical pursuit of rationality, which leads to the instrumentalisation of the mind against man. Most common motives used by the theory include fragmentation of identity, hyperreality, loss of cognitive bases and meta-narrative, the core meaning of discourse and language, and textualism (perception of reality through the prism of the metaphor of text)[47].

The postmodernist approach began spreading in management at the turn of the 1980s, influenced by the concepts of network society and consumerism. Authors who have used the postmodernist approach in management include S. Brown[48], F. A. Firat, J. Clifford, I. Shultz[49], A. Yenkatesh, M.B. Holbrook[50] and J. Oglivy[51].

---

44 I. Szmigin, M. Carrigan, 'New Consumption Communities: Resisting the Hegemony of the Marketing Process', in: 3rd *International Critical Management Studies Conference*, Lancaster, 2003.

45 C. Bekin, 'Research Ethics and Fieldwork at New Consumption Communities', in: *4th International Critical Management Studies Conference*, Lancaster, 2004.

46 P. Engholm, *The Controversy Between Modernist and Postmodernist Views of Management Science: Is a Synergy Possible?* Internet, Monash University, May 2001; D.M. Boje, R.P. Jr Gephart, T.J. Thatchenkery, *Postmodern Management and Organization Theory,* Sage Publications, Thousand Oaks, 1996; M.K. Welge, D. Holtbrugge, 'International Management Under Postmodern Conditions', *Management International Review*, vol. 39, no. 4, 1999, pp. 305-322; G. Burrell, R. Cooper, 'Modernism, Postmodernism and Organizational Analysis: An Introduction', *Organization Studies*, vol. 9, no. 1, 1998, pp. 91-112.

47 M. Alvesson, S. Deetz, 'Critical Theory and Postmodernism: Approaches to Organization Studies', in: *Critical Management Studies. A Reader*, Ch. Grey, H. Willmott (eds.), Oxford University Press, New York, 2005.

48 S. Brown, 'Postmodern Marketing', *European Journal of Marketing*, no. 27 (4), 1993, pp. 19-34.

Interplay beetween paradigms

Neoevolutionism in the social sciences is undoubtedly a proposal of a new paradigm. It is therefore worth answering the question: what are the connections of this cognitive perspective with other paradigms? Is neoevolutionism a radical departure from all the basic cognitive assumptions that characterise the various paradigms of the social sciences?

When looking for a social sciences paradigm that would be closest to neoevolutionism, one can point to functionalism. It originates from the epistemological assumptions of neopositivism, and therefore, itself assumes objectivism of cognition, realism and empiricism, verificationism and falsificationism, as the criteria of science. Functionalism seeks to improve the standard of scientific research through methods modelled on the natural sciences. The classic functionalist image of social institutions and human nature assumes the adaptive function of human behaviour and shares some features with neoevolutionism. Functionalism, however, does not take into account the assumption that the human brain, based on the coupling of the genes and environment, is accustomed to dealing with the core issues of the survival and reproduction of individuals from the distant past, and not from the present time. The "troglodyte" brain has a range of mechanisms that are not functional from the point of view of the present time, e.g. a tendency to gorge on the most caloric products led to the survival of primates, whereas nowadays it is harmful. In accordance with the assumptions of neoevolutionism, most functionalists largely overestimate the role of culture in the formation of the social world and underestimate genetic conditions. There are also no explanations as to the importance of reproduction, which from the point of view of the egoism of genes is the most crucial criterion, more important even than survival.

Indubitably, neoevolutionism differs significantly from the symbolic-interpretive paradigm, both on the epistemological and methodological level. Interpretivism assumes subjectivism or intersubjectivism of cognition, dualism and essentialism, and certain methodology based on hermeneutics and phenomenology. In addition to the obvious opposition of the two paradigms, one

---

49 A. Firat, A. Fuat, C. J. Shultz, 'From Segmentation to Fragmentation: Markets and Market Strategy in the Postmodern Era', *European Journal of Marketing*, no. 31 (3/4), 1997, pp. 183-207; A. Firat, A. Fuat, A. Yenkatesh, 'Postmodernity: The age of marketing', *International Journal of Research in Marketing*, no. 10, 1993, pp. 227-249.

50 B.M. Holbrook, 'The Three Faces of Elitism: Postmodernism, Political Correctness, and Popular Culture', *Journal of Macromarketing*, no. 15 (Fall), 1995, pp. 128-163.

51 J. Oglivy, 'The Postmodern Business', *Marketing and Research Today*, no. 18 (1), 1990, pp. 4-20.

can also find slightly deeper similarities. The vision of man in interpretivism departs from the overly rationalised assumptions of Homo oeconomicus, which are quite visible in functionalism. Man, entangled in the network of meaning and sense, which he himself creates, is based on complex emotional and intellectual motives and is not internally uniform[52]. Interpretivism also considers the influence of psychoanalysis and the discovery of the subconscious. It seems that neoevolutionism is far from over-rationalising the image of the human mind, which stems from the questioning of the Cartesian tradition of the knowing subject. As part of its nature, Homo sapiens have natural instincts related to reproduction, survival, social life etc. However, the evolutionary redundancy of the human brain (exaptation[53]) leads to the creation of higher needs. Consequently, the brain connects various and sometimes contradictory needs and motives on different levels of the conscious and unconscious. Description of human behaviours cannot therefore overestimate the rational sphere and overlook cognitive illusions of not always functional emotions and instinctive actions.

Neoevolutionism is clearly contradictory to the radical structuralism paradigm. In accordance with the assumptions of neoevolutionism, the critical theory is not a theory in the scientific sense, but an ideology. The assumption about the involvement of the knowing subject in the process of change and the pursuit of the emancipation change, combined with the rejection of the neopositivist epistemology, are completely antagonistic to neoevolutionism. The only common element of the two paradigms seems to be the disillusioned vision of human nature and society.

Radical structuralism interprets the social world in egoistical categories. People seek power, property, control over resources, and fulfilment of their needs. Society and culture are extensions of these tendencies. Social institutions are oppressive, use symbolic violence or produce a false collective awareness, which equates to maintaining an unjust order. Disruption of the status quo is a revolutionary action, which requires the involvement of disadvantaged social groups. Similarly to radical structuralism, neoevolutionism suggests egoistical motives of individuals, which are limited by the social nature of man.

“Programming” by genes results in susceptibility to: idealisation of oneself, rationalisation of one’s negative actions, and nepotism. In neoevolutionism, even altruism is not selfless. By saving one’s relatives, they save their own genes; through cooperation with strangers, they increase their chances for

---

52 C. Geertz, *The Interpretation of Cultures,* Basic Books, New York, 1973.

53 S. Nowak, *Metodologia badań społecznych,* Wydawnictwo Naukowe PWN, Warsaw, 2007, p. 262.

survival and reproduction. By way of consolation, it can only be added that neither neoevolutionism nor the critical theory heads towards this egoistical determinism. Genetic "programming" is never complete and is just a tendency, not behavioural automatism. It is therefore possible to overcome biological pressure, which is proved by many people on a daily basis, e.g. when they decide to adopt children. Also the existence of the two paradigms is a proof of human emancipation from biological and political mechanisms.

There is a chasm between radical humanism, sometimes identified with postmodernism, and neoevolutionism. Postmodernism is subjectivist and relativist, and simultaneously sceptical towards science. Neoevolutionism, on the other hand, displays objectivist orientation, seeks generalisation and universalism in cognition, and has a great dose of trust for scientific institutions.

Summary

In opposition, the standard model of the social sciences versus neoevolutionism does not seem entirely true. In reality, although it proposes a radical change of cognitive perspective in the social sciences, neoevolutionism maintains a more complex interrelation with other paradigms of the social sciences. In terms of the philosophy of science, it refers mostly to neopositivism, although its vision of the human mind is far from the rationalism and empiricism of the Vienna Circle. From among the four paradigms of the social sciences, neoevolutionism seems closest to functionalism. Although most neoevolutionary assumptions do not comply with the symbolic-interpretive paradigm, there are some common areas, such as those related to the vision of Homo sociologicus, bounded rationality and the barriers to interpretation and cognitive illusions. Neoevolutionism is in clear opposition to subjectivist paradigms, by completely rejecting radical structuralism and humanism and postmodernist approaches that are based on radical epistemological relativism.

Neoevolutionism seems to be a very promising direction of research, which uses not only theory with various levels of detail, but also developed research methods. Cognitively valuable is its provision of important arguments supporting the monistic stand in epistemology, according to which the social reality and human mind can be examined by means of the same assumptions and similar methods as nature. In my opinion, however, too radical a stand in relation to other paradigms and theories is not necessary. Apart from the philosophical core and methods derived from the natural sciences, neoevolutionism also uses ideas and methodology developed in the social sciences. A certain dose of epistemological pluralism that, clearly, does not involve radical cognitive relativists, should be therefore conducive to the development of the paradigm.

Chapter 2
Development of evolutionary thought – from social Darwinism to behavioral economics

Introduction

Evolutionism in the social sciences has many meanings. Most visible is the dichotomy between literal and metaphorical understanding of the application of evolution to theories and research on the human mind, society and culture. The literal interpretation uses concepts of the influence of the biologically shaped human nature on the functioning of the society and culture. The metaphorical one refers to the creation of a sequential theory of social development that is modelled on the biological evolution. Both interpretations derive from the historical trend of social Darwinism, which hypothesised about the human nature and proposed a theoretical system. Nowadays, the literal understanding of evolution in the social sciences is mainly presented by evolutionary psychology and sociobiology, although elements of the approach can also be found in other disciplines, such as behavioural economics and evolutionary anthropology. The metaphorical understanding of evolution is popular in all social sciences. Theories of development that use evolution as a metaphor were proposed by both 19th century and contemporary researchers: sociologists Auguste Comte, Ferdinand Tönnies, Talcott Parsons; economists Joseph Schumpeter and Kurt Dopfer; anthropologists James George Frazer and Lewis Henry Morgan[54].

The subject of interest of this chapter is, most of all, the literal understanding of the theory of evolution in the social sciences. The analysis of the achievements of modern neoevolutionism in several social sciences will serve as a foundation for the programme of a new research field, combining the problems of organisation and management with neoevolutionism, evolutionary psychology and behavioural economics.

---

54 A. Comte, *A General View of Positivism,* Heinemann, London, 1856; F. Tönnies, *Wspólnota i stowarzyszenie. Rozprawa o komunizmie i socjalizmie jako empirycznych formach kultury,* PWN, Warsaw, 1988; T. Parsons, *Societies: Evolutionary and Comparative Perspectives,* Prentice-Hall, Englewood Cliffs NJ, 1966; J.A. Schumpeter, *Capitalism, Socialism and Democracy,* Routledge, London, 1994; K. Dopfer, *The Evolutionary Foundations of Economics,* Cambridge University Press, Cambridge, 2005, pp. 391-430; J.G. Frazer, *Złota gałąź. Studia z magii i religii,* Wyd. KR, Warsaw, 2002; L.H. Morgan, R. Fox, *Ancient Society,* Transaction Publishers, 2000.

History of evolutionism in the social sciences

The history of evolutionism in the social sciences began with the publication of Charles Darwin's *On the Origin of Species* and later *The Descent of Man*. However, it was H. Spencer who created the theory of social Darwinism, together with the slogan "survival of the fittest"[55]. Using the concept of evolution as a point of reference for sociological, psychological, anthropological, economical and political theories was quite popular from the second half of the 19th century to World War II. At the beginning of the 20th century, however, social evolutionism began to be criticised from the perspective of functionalism, mainly in sociology and anthropology. Most of the evolutionary hypotheses by H. Spencer, W.G. Sumner and L.H. Morgan were not confirmed by ethnological research on primitive societies[56].

Evolutionism also became a theory, and formed the basis for eugenics, a pseudoscience whose assumptions were formed in 1883 by F. Galton[57]. Eugenics, which transformed into an influential social and political movement within a few decades, postulated selection of the best genes in the society through limiting the possibility for reproduction of individuals with "low quality" genes (negative selection) and facilitating the reproduction of the carriers of "high quality" genetic material (positive selection). Eugenics became the key, pseudoscientific justification for racism and Nazi genocide. The grim past of theories that use the rules of natural selection in man's social and political life became the fundamental cause for the rejection of Darwin's theory in the social sciences after World War II, and the objection that met the attempts to reactivate social evolutionism in the form of sociobiology.

Sociobiology

The name for the discipline was suggested in 1975, by Edward O. Wilson, in his *Sociobiology: The New Synthesis*[58]. In an ideological manner, and supported by relatively weak empirical evidence, the work predicted the development of sociology based on biology, and future integration of research results with economics and cultural anthropology. By diagnosing the state of sociobiology as a science in development, E.O. Wilson suggested that it held certain empirical

---

55 H. Spencer, *Principles of Biology,* Williams & Norgate, London, 1864.

56 W.G. Sumner, *On Liberty, Society, and Politics: The Essential Essays of William Graham Sumner,* ed. R.C. Bannister (Indianapolis: Liberty Fund, 1992). online

57 F. Galton, *Inquiries into Human Faculty and its Development,* Macmillan, London, 1883.

58 E.O. Wilson, *Sociobiology: The New Synthesis* 1975, Harvard University Press, 2000.

material on human social behaviours, however it had not yet created a system that would bring together dispersed facts in an adequate manner[59].

When analysing the most important assumptions of sociobiology, one can point out many assumptions that deal with its programme, methodology and epistemic ideals. Most of all, in the epistemological sphere it is neopositivism that assumes scientific realism, objectivism, verificationism and the use of methods from the natural sciences. The programme is based on biological reductionism in the explanation of social processes, whose fundament is a search for genetic conditions of human behaviours (genetic determinism)[60].

Despite controversies around the radicalism of sociobiology, Wilson's suggestions concerning the possibility of explaining human behaviour by means of evolutionary models proved largely correct. However the development of the programme in evolutionary research on social life determinants was realised in disciplines other than sociology, mainly in evolutionary psychology, neuroscience and cognitive science. The reactions of many sociologists and other representatives of the social science to Wilson's sociobiology were intense, negative and very emotional. They pointed out biological and genetic determinism, elimination of human conciousness, and suppression of morality and ethics to the biological level[61]. Culturalism[62], rooted in sociology, dominated over sociobiology, which in its initial phase was empirically weak. Sociobiology was rejected by most sociologists not only because of their fear of biological determinism and the taboo of anthropocentrism, but also through the negation of the traditional assumptions of sociology and the rejection of most of its theoretical achievements[63]. Fear of returning to social Darwinism, eugenics, and their destructive consequences from the past, obscured the value of the new perspective. Historical reasons, therefore, prevented sociobiology from becoming a paradigm. Instead, it remained a niche subdiscipline, involved in social and ideological disputes. In hindsight, it might be that the revolutionary postulates of sociobiology led to sociology's departure from its alliance with evolutionism, and to the growing importance of postmodernist trends that promoted epistemological and cultural relativism.

In reaction to such harsh criticism, the radicalism of sociobiological postulates was softened thanks to a proposal to connect perspectives of the

---

59 Ibid., pp. 321-323.

60 Ibid., p. 322.

61 U. Segerstråle, *Defenders of the Truth: the Sociobiology Debate,* Oxford University Press, London, 2001, pp. 13-34.

62 S. Pinker, *Tabula rasa. Spory o naturę ludzką,* GWP, Gdańsk, 2005.

63 B. Szacka, J. Szacki (eds.), *Człowiek, zwierzę społeczne,* , Czytelnik, Warsaw, 1991, pp. 194-195.

social sciences with evolutionary biology. P.L. van den Berghe discovered possibilities for the integration of evolutionism with economics, the social exchange theory, the game theory, behaviourism, and – on a 'macro' level – with Marxism and some versions of functionalism. Many sociobiologists accepted the need for research on social and cultural processes that cannot be reduced to the biological level[64]. In the 1980s, sociobiology was largely ostracised by the environment of the social sciences; evolutionary psychology became a discipline that used the neoevolutionary synthesis in the empirical sphere in the social sciences.

Evolutionary psychology

Evolutionism is simultaneously the oldest and the youngest cognitive perspective in psychology. The oldest attempts to use evolutionary explanations in psychology began as early as in the 19th century, with Charles Darwin[65]. Until the end of World War II psychology was relatively often used to explain mental processes. Over the following few dozen years, however, psychologists reluctantly referred to Darwinism, bearing in mind the consequences of the social Darwinist ideology. New stimuli for the development of evolutionary psychology were the completion of work on the neoevolutionary synthesis, which took place in the 1960s and 1970s, the creation of sociobiology and development of neuroscience and cognitivism, together with the use of new techniques of brain examination[66].

Rapid development of evolutionary psychology began in the 1980s, mainly thanks to research on human behaviour. Several authors also attempted to formulate a paradigm for the developing discipline[67]. Nowadays, it is more and more common to think that evolutionary psychology proposes an image of

---

64 P.L. van den Berghe, 'Łączenie paradygmatów: biologia i nauki społeczne', in: *Człowiek, zwierzę społeczne,* ibid., p. 203.

65 C. Darwin, *The Descent of Man, and Selection in Relation to Sex*, (1st ed.) London: John Murray, 1871.

66 R.L. Trivers, 'The Evolution of Reciprocal Altruism', *The Quarterly Review of Biology*, 1971; W.D. Hamilton, 'Innate Social Aptitudes of Man: An Approach from Evolutionary Genetics', in: *Biosocial Anthropology,* R. Fox (ed.), Malaby Press, London, 1975, pp. 133-153.

67 J. Tooby, L. Cosmides, 'Toward Mapping the Evolved Functional Organization of Mind and Brain', in: *The New Cognitive Neuroscience,* M. Gazzaniga (ed.), MIT Press, Cambridge Mass., 2000; D.M. Buss, *Evolutionary Psychology. The New Science of the Mind,* Pearson, Boston, 2008.

human nature that will become a basis for the integration of various disciplines of science[68].

When analysing the most important assumptions of psychology, one can point out epistemological and methodological assumptions, the preferred methodology, assumptions related to the human nature and behaviour, and research questions. The epistemological postulates deal mainly with bringing psychology closer to the scientific standards of the natural sciences, e.g. evolutionary biology. In the sphere of cognitive philosophy, this means scientific realism, pursuit of objective cognition, the ideal of mathematical modelling and moderate verificationism or falsificationism[69].

A scientific method involves the use of a social experiment, which is rooted in psychology, with the assumptions of randomisation and control of the variables. Evolutionary psychology does not reject methods from other related disciplines, such as: neuroscience (brain examination), cognitivism (analysis of human cognitive skills), sociology (survey research), primatology (observation of primate behaviour), and palaeoanthropology (interpretation of hominid behaviour based on archaeological findings). Evolutionary psychologists' view of human nature is based on the antithesis of the idea of *tabula rasa*. According to J. Tooby and L. Cosmides, the human nature is a system of mental modules formed in the process of the evolution of hominids and *Homo sapiens* (in the Pleistocene), which serve to solve problems of the survival and reproduction of individuals[70]. This is why the canon of human behaviours includes behavioural models related to: reactions to fight or flight, discovering social scamps, sexual demonstration, and search for and consumption of food. A special role is played by modules and models of social behaviour that most probably became key to the survival of individuals, and set a direction for rapid changes of hominids. Significant researchers in evolutionary psychology include: J. Tooby and L. Cosmides, D. M. Buss, S. Pinker, R. Dunbar, L. Burnett, P. Ekman and D. Kenrick[71].

The assumptions of evolutionary psychology are: the modularity of the mind, the search for psychological evolutionary mechanisms, and analysis of

68 R. Dunbar, L. Barrett, 'Evolutionary Psychology in the Round', in: R.I.M. Dunbar, L. Barrett, *Evolutionary Psychology,* Oxford University Press, New York, 2007.

69 S. Psillos, *Scientific Realism: How Science Tracks Truth,* Routledge, London, 1999.

70 J. Tooby, L. Cosmides, 'Toward Mapping the Evolved Functional Organization of Mind and Brain', in: *The New Cognitive Neuroscience,* M.S. Gazzaniga (ed.), MIT Press, Cambridgc Mass., 2000.

71 R. Dunbar, L. Barrett, *Oxford Handbook of Evolutionary Psychology,* Oxford University Press, Oxford, 2007.

human social nature and diversity between various groups of people[72]. Evolutionary psychology is currently very rapidly developing trend in psychology. On the one hand, the discipline has its roots in evolutionism and on the other, in experimental achievements in psychology. By drawing conclusions from the negative experience of sociobiology, the creators of evolutionary psychology have made it a clearly empirical discipline, and tried to dissociate themselves from any ideological interpretations. Great empirical achievements of the last half a century makes it possible to describe human nature and behaviour on the basis of neoevolutionary assumptions. Now though, it is time for other disciplines of the social sciences to draw conclusions.

Cultural anthropology and paleoanthropology

Anthropology is a discipline, whose split into antagonistic paradigms is clearly visible. On the one hand, there is a strong trend of evolutionary anthropology and paleoanthropology, which postulates the use of methods from the natural sciences (archaeology, genetics and ethology) and ethnology for research on the evolution of the human species and culture. On the other, the role of the interpretive paradigm and postmodernist views is also very important, which postulate cultural or epistemological relativism. Evolutionists question the cognitive value of research by interpretivists and postmodernists, while the latter support the autonomy of the humanist sciences from the natural sciences, indicating the ideological scientism, reductionism and epistemological fundamentalism of evolutionary anthropology. Most anthropologists are sceptical of the possibility of reaching a consensus between the two perspectives.

From the point of view of scientific value, one should differentiate between interpretive and postmodernist views in anthropology. The symbolic-interpretive paradigm has developed numerous qualitative cognitive methods, which can improve the understanding of culture. In addition, it seems possible to combine the interpretive methodology with the neoevolutionary methodology on the grounds of pluralism or epistemological eclecticism[73]. Postmodernist discourse largely renounces scientific ambitions and instead focuses on cultural studies.

---

72 cf. D.M. Buss, *Evolutionary Psychology. The New Science of the Mind*, Pearson, Boston, 2008, pp. 36-69.

73 Ł. Sułkowski, *Epistemologia w naukach o zarządzaniu,* PWE, Warsaw, 2005, pp. 165-168.

Paleoanthropology uses archaeological methods that enable the identification and description of the paths of development of human culture, and which are versions of a broader theory of cultural evolution[74].

Behavioural economics

The evolutionary metaphor has been broadly used in economics, for example in the analyses by Joseph Schumpeter, Thorstein Veblen, Kurt Dopfer and Ulrich Witt. Evolutionary assumptions of selection, changeability and reproduction have been used in relation to economic entities and the economic market. This has led to the use of a range of biological terms that were related to population ecology and balance. Contemporary researchers who use evolutionary analogies in economics are usually aware of cognitive limitations that result from the transfer of biological terms to the social sciences discourse[75].

A relatively new trend that uses evolutionary psychology is behavioural psychology, which derives from the alliance of economics with cognitive psychology. The originators of the discipline are believed to be A. Tversky and Nobel Prize winner D. Kahneman. Behavioural economics operates on the level of microeconomics and focuses on the research on conditions for economic decision-making by man. Key research questions concern the search for a decision-making model under conditions of uncertainty, the analyses of perceptive and cognitive illusions, and interpretation of man's economic behaviour in the categories of evolutionary cognitive models. The trend's methodology is based mainly on social experiments but also uses statistical, demographical and historical analyses[76]. Thanks to the use of brain examination techniques, it is currently possible to examine, among other things, the neuronal bases of decision-making. Apart from behavioural economics, there also exists a related and developing branch of behavioural finance, which deals with psychological conditions for financial decision-making.

Behavioural economics straddles the line between economics and psychology. It deals with many problems that are also a subject of the management sciences (e.g. organisational behaviour) and sociology. The trend's

---

74 S. Shennan, 'Evolutionary Perspectives in Archaeology: From Culture History to Cultural Evolution', in: R.I.M. Dunbar, L. Barrett, *Evolutionary Psychology,* Oxford University Press, New York, 2007.

75 K. Dopfer, *Evolutionary Economics. Program and Scope,* Kluwer Academic Publishers, Boston, 2001, pp. 1–44; U. Witt, 'Evolutionary economics', *The new Palgrave Dictionary of Economics,* 2nd Ed., v. 3, London, 2008, pp. 67-68.

76 C.F. Camerer, G. Loewenstein, M. Rabin (eds.), *Advances in Behavioral Economics*, Princeton University Press, Princeton NJ, 2001, pp. 7-8.

development confirms the openness of economics, as a scientific discipline, to new theoretical and empirical inspirations.

The idea of bounded rationality was introduced to the economic discourse by Herbert Simon[77], although relations between behavioural economics and evolutionism are very modern and involve the search for evolutionary and cognitive sources of economic behaviour[78]. Bounded rationality examines, for example, evolutionary conditions for risk aversion[79] and the question of trust and reciprocity[80]. According to G.. Loewenstein, however, evolutionary conditions cannot be the sole variable that is taken into consideration while making conscious economic decisions[81].

Evolutionary management?

The management sciences use the evolutionary metaphor quite often. In sequential theories of the development of economic entities, a market is compared to the environment, and an economic entity to individuals or species[82]. In the trend of population ecology, sectors and markets are compared

77 H. Simon, 'A Behavioral Model of Rational Choice', *The Quarterly Journal of Economics*, vol. 69, no. 1, 1955, pp. 99-118.

78 D. Kahneman, A. Tversky, 'Prospect Theory: An Analysis of Decision under Risk', *Econometrica* 47 (2), 1979, pp. 263-291; S. Hersh, *Beyond Greed and Fear: Understanding Behavioral Finance and the Psychology of Investing,* Oxford University Press, New York, 2002.

79 B. Winterhalder, 'Risk and Decision-Making', in: R.I.M. Dunbar, L. Barrett, *Evolutionary Psychology*, Oxford University Press, New York, 2007; L. Carmichael, W.B. MacLeod, *Fair Territory: Preferences, Bargaining, and the Endowment Effect,* Queen's University, Mimeo, 1999.

80 E. Fehr, K.M. Schmidt, 'A Theory of Fairness, Competition, and Cooperation', *Quarterly Journal of Economics*, vol. 114, no. 3, 1999, pp. 817-868; E. Fehr, 'On The Economics and Biology of Trust', *Journal of the European Economic Association*, vol. 7, no. 2-3, 2009, pp. 235-266; A. Falk, E. Fehr, Ch. Zehnder, 'Fairness Perceptions and Reservation Wages—The Behavioral Effects of Minimum Wage Laws', *Quarterly Journal of Economics*, vol. 121, no. 4, 2006, pp. 1347-1381; E. Fehr, J.A. List, 'The Hidden Costs and Returns of Incentives-Trust and Trustworthiness Among CEOs', *Journal of the European Economic Association*, vol. 2, no. 5, 2004, pp. 743-771.

81 *Advances in Behavioral Economics,* op. cit., pp. 46-47.

82 J. Freeman, 'Organizational Life Cycles and Natural Selection Processes', in: *Research in Organizational Behaviour,* B.M. Staw, L.L. Cummings (eds.), JAI Press, Greenwich, 1968.

to the natural environment[83]. Adaptation to the environment is used as a point of reference in strategic management[84]. Change management uses the dichotomous classification: evolutionary change – revolutionary change[85].

All the quoted examples of the use of evolution in management refer to its metaphorical understanding. The literal interpretation of evolution is practically absent in the management sciences. Behavioural finance identifies more with the problems of economics. A few exceptions involve isolated works on the use of evolutionary psychology in human resource management and marketing[86]. There is an obvious gap in the development of the theory and methodology of the discipline, if compared to psychology, economics, sociology and anthropology. There are several probable reasons for the gap in the development of the evolutionary approach in the management sciences.

Firstly, disciplines that are more established institutionally and academically took an interest in the problems of the evolutionary conditions of management. As an example we can quote the problem of management decision-making used in behavioural economics. Secondly, contrary to psychology, the methodology of the management sciences is not based on the method of social experimentation and has not used brain examination techniques. One exception here could be the first programmes for research on decision-making, from the marketing perspective[87]. Thirdly, from the point of view of the development of modern sciences, it is often more important to creatively use a certain research field than to place it among institutional disciplines of science. In this understanding, for instance, research on the evolutionary aversion to risky decisions or unconscious motives for purchase of consumer goods, related to our species' past, form problems that can be solved by means of scientific methods. These derive from various disciplines, which might be one of the reasons for their innovative character. Fourthly, the reason for the absence of the theory of

---

83 J. Pfeffer, G.R. Galancik, *The External Control of Organizations: A Resource Dependence Perspective,* Harper and Row, New York, 1978; E.L. Trist, 'A Concept of Organizational Ecology', *Australia Journal of Management*, no. 2, 1976.

84 K.E. Weick, *Managing the Unexpected,* Jossey-Bass, San Francisco CA, 2001.

85 H. Aldrich, *Organizations and Environments,* Prentice-Hall, Englewood Cliffs NJ, 1979.

86 N. Nicholson, 'Evolutionary Psychology: Toward a New View of Human Nature and Organizational Society', *Human Relations*, Springer Netherlands, vol. 50, no. 9/September, 1997; G. Saad, T. Gill, 'Applications of Evolutionary Psychology in Marketing', *Psychology & Marketing,* John Wiley & Sons, vol. 17 (12), 2000, pp. 1005-1034.

87 This refers to so-called neuromarketing. See: M. Lindstrom, *Buyology: Truth and Lies about why We Buy*, Doubleday Business, New York, 2008.

evolution in management is lack of the awareness of the potential of the neoevolutionary synthesis. Most specialists in the field of management at first glance fail to notice a relation between our biological heritage and solutions to the key questions of effective organisation and management. How then, can the neoevolutionary trend be used in the management sciences?

It seems that neoevolutionism can be beneficial to researchers and practitioners of organisation and management in terms of proposing a coherent paradigm to explain human behaviour, providing detailed behavioural theories related to organisation, proposing an innovative research methodology and pragmatic management techniques[88].

Neoevolutionism is a paradigm that is based on neopositivist models of scientific realism, objectivism and reductionism. Its core is formed by the theory of the evolution of man's cognitive and behavioural mechanisms, which is the foundation for explaining, predicting and describing human behaviour. In this understanding, management can administer a new paradigm, different to those previously used, which is the basis for the integration of the management sciences with other social and natural sciences on a higher epistemological level.

Detailed behavioural theories refer to the modelling of various areas of human behaviour that are crucial in management. Nowadays, foundations for middle range social theories are being created which accept evolutionary conditions and deal with, for instance, motivation, leadership, exercising power, relations between the sexes, family relations, purposeful action and planning, altruism and cooperation, and creation of cultural models. These will provide revised concepts based on experimental research, which will replace some of the old concepts (e.g. A. Maslow's hierarchy of needs and M. Weber's theory of charismatic management and bureaucracy[89]). From the point of view of such areas of management as: human resource management, organisational behaviours, organisational culture, and organisational structure and strategies, this leads to the formation of completely new theories of organisation and management.

Similarly to evolutionary psychology and behavioural economics, management can use experimental methods more broadly. For solving management problems, traditional experiment, typical for social psychology, and techniques for brain analysis, for instance in decision-making processes, and emotions and perception assessment can all be useful. This does not mean, of

---

88 Ł. Sułkowski, *Management on the Neoevolutionary Foundations*, "Organizacja i Kierowanie. Organization and Management" , no 1 (139), p. 23-44.

89 A. Maslow, *A Theory of Human Motivation* (originally published in *Psychological Review*, 1943, Vol. 50 #4, pp. 370–396

course, that previous methods have been abandoned. On the contrary, the pluralist approach, which assumes the possibility of combining statistical, documentation, survey, and observation methods (both quantitative and qualitative) with experimental methods, should result in interesting cognitive effects.

In the pragmatic sphere, the neoevolutionary theory of management should, over time, result in the application of organisational methods and techniques, which are conducive to greater effectiveness. The above-mentioned areas of motivation, leadership and organisational culture can then gain new techniques thanks to the neoevolutionary vision of human nature and social organisation.

Summary

Disciplines of the social sciences can be analysed from the point of view of the degree of utilisation, absorption and the specificity of the evolutionary approach. In psychology, the evolutionary approach belongs to the main trend and develops dynamically, both in the theoretical and empirical sphere. In economics, the literal interpretation of the theory of evolution refers mainly to the behavioural trend, which straddles several disciplines. Sociology largely rejected the radical sociobiological proposal; the literal evolutionary approach is currently rather marginal in this discipline. In anthropology, the evolutionary trend is significant, mainly thanks to paleoanthropological research and comparative intercultural studies.

It seems that the development of neoevolutionary research and theory in the management sciences can have many cognitive advantages. However, using the experience of other disciplines, it is worth attempting to realise a research programme based on a moderate neoevolutionary approach. The experience of sociobiology and, earlier, neopositivism in the philosophy of cognition indicates that radical, reductionist programmes for the introduction of the theory and methodology of the natural sciences in the social sciences are doomed to failure. The complex world of culture, society and mind requires the use of the greatest possible number of valuable cognitive methods. A research programme that combines experimental methods with other methods of the social sciences could lead to the development of valuable organisation and management theories in the future.

Chapter 3
Management from the perspective of Darwinism

Introduction

Darwin's theory of evolution is a fundamental and established philosophy and methodology of the biological sciences, which deserves to be called a paradigm. Early attempts to use the paradigm in the social sciences, however, were not successful. In the 19th century, the concept of the survival of the fittest in society became a synonym with Herbert Spencer's social evolutionism, which subsequent generations of the idea being immediately associated with discrimination and even the Nazi ideology[90]. In the 20th century, indignation finally met the social interpretations of Wilson's sociobiology, which led to the reduction of humanities and the social sciences to genetic and biological bases. The assumptions of R. Dawkins' memetics were similarly met with a great dose of scepticism[91].

It seems, however, that faced with the incredibly dynamic development of the empirical research based on the evolutionary paradigm, which helps explain many complex behaviours of organisms, including people, it is worthwhile giving Darwinism a second chance in the social sciences. After all, this new perspective is already proposed by many contemporary disciplines of science, including very young disciplines such as evolutionary psychology, sociobiology, cognitivism, primatology, artificial intelligence (AI) and neuroscience. By combining experience in research on human behaviour of social and humanist disciplines, with the evolutionary paradigm and modern methods of brain examination, it is possible to significantly dynamise research in the social sciences[92].

A crucial cognitive condition for the development of this interdisciplinary alliance is the transfer of the evolutionary paradigm to the social sciences. In psychology, we observe a rapid development of the approach called evolutionary psychology, which is an answer to the criticism of orthodox

---

90 H. Spencer, *Principles of Biology,* University Press of the Pacific, vol. 1, 1864, p. 444, after: M.E. Stucke, *Better Competition Advocacy,* http://works.bepress.com/cgi/cgi?article=1000&context=maurice_stucke.

91 S.J. Gould, R. Lewontin, *The Spandrels of San Marco and the Panglossion Paradigm: A Critique of the Adaptationist Programme,* London, 1979, B 205, pp. 581-598.

92 C. Elworthy, *Homo Biologicus. An Evolutionary Model for the Human Sciences,* Duncker & Humblot, Berlin, Internet 1993, accessed 2007.

sociobiology[93]. Much greater are the controversies related to the application of evolutionism in sociology and cultural anthropology. From the point of view of the management sciences, it might seem that research on the evolutionary trend is very distant from organisational problems. Closer analysis, however, shows that accepting evolutionary explanations affects the functioning of all sciences devoted to human behaviour (behavioural sciences).

The aim of the chapter is to outline the perspective of how the modern evolutionary concept influences the management sciences. It searches for the sources of organisational and management processes in the biological and social character of *Homo sapiens*. Thanks to Darwinist inspirations, it has become possible to better understand human behaviour in organisations[94].

Neoevolutionism and human behaviour

The theory of evolution shows a fundamental mechanism of species to be that of adaptation, through random and accumulated change, to conditions of the environment. The theory of genetic inheritance was created much later and enabled a coherent explanation of the mechanism of reproduction and genetic change (mutation)[95]. In 1964, William D. Hamilton described the theory of evolution from the perspective of gene distribution, indicating not only the reproduction of genes through offspring but also kin selection[96]. This enabled the explanation of kin altruism, as a fundamental mechanism in the nature. In the 1970s, Robert Trivers proposed evolutionary theories explaining non-kin reciprocal altruism, the concept of parental investment and conflict between parents and their offspring[97].

In 1975, Edward O. Wilson published his book *Sociobiology: The New Synthesis*, described the state of contemporary evolutionism, which enabled

93 J. Tooby, L. Cosmides, 'Toward Mapping the Evolved Functional Organization of Mind and Brain', in: *The New Cognitive Neuroscience*, M. Gazzaniga (ed.), MIT Press, Cambridge Mass., 2000, pp. 1167-1178.

94 B.D. Pierce, R. White, 'The Evolution of Social Structure: Why Biology Matters', *Academy of Management Review*, vol. 24, 1999, pp. 843-853.

95 W. Bateson, *Mendel 's Principles of Heredity, a Defense,* Cambridge University Press, London, 1902; Online Facsimile Edition: Electronic Scholarly Publishing, prepared by Robert Robbins.

96 W.D. Hamilton, 'The Genetical Evolution of Social Behaviour', *Journal of Theoretical Biology*, no. 7, 1964, pp. 1-52.

97 R.L. Trivers, 'The Evolution of Reciprocal Altruism', *Quarterly Review of Biology*, no. 46, 1971, pp. 35-57.

accurate interpretation and prediction of behaviour in the biological world[98]. A great controversy was, however, stirred by the book's final chapter, which applied the concept to human behaviour. It consisted mainly of hypotheses and not the results of empirical research, which invited attack not only from the ideological but also methodological point of view. The concepts of the explanation of human behaviour from the evolutionary perspective became a subject of evolutionary psychology and intense research of the last three decades, enabling the creation of a coherent theory of human behaviour based on evolutionary character[99].

The neoevolutionary synthesis combines the concept of natural and sexual selection with the idea of gene replication[100]. This might be characterised by the assumptions of:

- The natural selection of behaviours, which assumes that in the long-term perspective of the survival of *Homo sapiens*, those structures and behaviours have survived which are conducive to survival of an individual of the species, whereas non-functional structures and behaviours have gradually disappeared (this excludes behaviours leading to reproductive superiority);
- The sexual selection of behaviours, which assumes that in the long-term perspective of the survival of *Homo sapiens*, those structures and behaviours have survived which increase the chance for individual reproduction, even if they are non-functional from the point of view of individual survival[101];
- The modularity of the mind, which assumes that in the human mind, and in the mind of earlier species, evolution has created specific structures whose function is to solve problems related to survival and reproduction[102];
- The theory of the "egoism of genes", which states that the core althought hidden motive for an individual's actions is genetic reproduction and

98 E.O. Wilson, *Sociobiology: The New Synthesis* 1975, Harvard University Press, 2000.

99 J. Tooby, L. Cosmides, *Toward Mapping the Evolved Functional Organization of Mind and Brain,* op. cit., pp. 1167-1178.

100 cf. L. Barrett, R. Dunbar, J. Lycett, *Human Evolutionary Psychology,* Palgrave Macmillan, New York, 2002, pp. 22-44; D.M. Buss, *Evolutionary Psychology. The New Science of the Mind,* Pearson, Boston, 2008, pp. 36-69.

101 G. Miller, *The Mating Mind: How Sexual Choice Shaped the Evolution of Human Nature,* Heinemann, London, 2000.

102 J.A. Fodor, *The Modularity of Mind: An Essay in Faculty Psychology,* MIT Press, Cambridge Mass., 1983; J. Barkow, L. Cosmides, J. Tooby, *The Adapted Mind: Evolutionary Psychology and the Generation of Culture,* Oxford University Press, Oxford, 1992.

distribution of one's genes, which is possible through offspring but also through helping kin reproduction based on a common genetic element[103];

- Kin mechanisms of development that result directly from the assumption of the "egoism of genes", and explain the question of parental care and investment, and kin altruism.

Contemporary evolutionism has become the dominant paradigm of the natural sciences, which has lead to coherent and verifiable explanations of human behaviours.

The assumptions of natural and sexual selection, and the egoism of genes make it possible to understand the specificity of human social nature, and are a challenge for the humanist sciences. On the basis of the neoevolutionary paradigm, several disciplines of science are rapidly developing, such as evolutionary psychology, neuroscience and cognitivism, and which straddle the line between biology and the social sciences.

Application of neoevolutionism in management

Evolutionism can serve as a basis for the explanation of many human collective behaviours which constitute the foundation of organisation and management processes. It is therefore worthwhile to look closely at potential uses of the paradigm and define further directions for research in the management sciences. These include a broad spectrum of social issues that are based on the evolutionary fundament, such as:

1. Biological roots of organisation;
2. Natural sources of the power structure;
3. Competition between individuals, conflict and fight for domination;
4. Organisation leadership;
5. Learning;
6. Group and organisational bonds;
7. Risk-taking;
8. Social communication;
9. Sexual behaviours;
10. Evolutionary conditions for the culture of societies and organisations.

103 D.S. Wilson, E.O. Wilson, 'Rethinking the Theoretical Foundations of Sociobiology', *The Quarterly Review of Biology*, no. 82 (4), 2007, pp. 327-348.

1. Biological roots of organisation

Organisational processes are rooted in human nature – most of our actions are of a social and organised character. As a social being, man is constituted by bonds and interactions with other people, which means that in the evolutionary process there evolves an organisational function that facilitates and optimises collective actions. Its creation requires acquisition by certain individuals of motivations and abilities that enable group work. These are passed on to an individual in the process of primary socialisation, by the family or a small social group. The assimilation of values, attitudes and models of behaviour is natural and happens through imitation or conditioning. To solve basic life problems related to food acquisition (hunting or gathering), protection and care for offspring, a primary group needs to cooperate.

On the basis of earlier evolutionary mechanisms of domination, cooperation and conflict, there evolves a group leadership, who make key decisions regarding the choice of right solutions, which enable survival and reproduction. The organisational function gains special meaning when individuals and groups meet less routine problems, for which ready-made solutions are not part of standard cultural models. This is when creative mechanisms are activated, whose creation involved a great evolutionary cost. Thanks to flexible and non-routine organisation, leadership and creativity, *Homo sapiens* can solve the most complex survival problems, in the most difficult, even very unstable conditions. It is not surprising, from the evolutionary point of view, that this social group has managed to populate the whole globe.

2. Natural sources of the power structure and hierarchy

Power and social hierarchy are not exclusive to the human world but are also popular in the animal kingdom. If by power one means the possibility to enforce one's will onto other individuals, then it is used by all primates and many other animal species. Hierarchy, reflected by the biological 'pecking order', is a statistical reflection of the accepted structure of power. Power and hierarchy play a special role in social species, since they put the leader not only in the dominant position, but also make him the decision-maker who no longer enforces his will onto isolated individuals but onto the whole social group. The consequences of such decisions are far more significant because they apply to all community members. Questions then arise that are related to power's emergence and legitimisation. The natural order assumes domination of the strongest but even in the case of chimpanzees, coalitions that put the power in the hands of the most socially competent or group individual are also common. From the functional perspective, it was essential for the realisation of long-term organisational projects not only to select the centre of power, but also to ensure its stability[104].

3. Competition between individuals, conflict and the fight for domination

Competition, conflict and the fight for domination are inseparable attributes of exercising power, which in social species can have very sophisticated forms. Competition is related to limited access to resources and unlimited needs for individual survival and reproduction. Fights and conflict can therefore be observed both between individuals and coalitions in a social group[105]. The complexity of competition processes and conflict requires analysis on many levels, which are related to problems of organisation and social games. Competition is therefore a mechanism for the development of individual and collective actions, which favours the use of both conflict and fighting, and cooperation to win in a social game.

4. Organisation leadership

Leadership, i.e. the emergence of an individual who makes decisions and enforces them in a group, is not exclusive to *Homo sapiens*. It is a functional solution which enables efficient realisation of the organisational function. It is crucial, however, to develop criteria for the emergence and maintenance of leadership, which are usually based on authority. In terms of indicating social respect and the readiness of group members to abide by the will of an individual, authority in the case of man is not a measure based solely on physical strength. Although domination in its physical or social sense could have existed in the species' past, and in its present might unconsciously be a condition that favours authority, more important are the ability to cooperate with a social group, which is based on communication, and the influence of a social model (ideal leader, image, reputation and respect). Evolutionary research on leadership and power is in its preliminary stage and mainly covers the search for mental modules that interfere in these social processes.

---

104 Ł. Sułkowski, *Universal Sources of Hierarchy and Power from the Perspective of Neo-evolutionism*, "Journal of Intercultural Management", Vol 1, Nr 2, 2009, p. 59-69.

105 A. Campbell, 'A Few Good Men: Evolutionary Psychology and Female Adolescent Aggression', in: *The Functional Mind. Readings in Evolutionary Psychology,* D.T. Ken-rick, CL. Luce (eds.), Pearson, Boston, 2004.

5. Learning and creativity in a social group

From the point of view of the management sciences, the processes of learning and cognition of reality are crucial, and are related to the creation of a cognitive model that would enable problem solving. As shown by rather advanced research in evolutionary psychology on the processes of learning, people as a species have a cognitive system which evolved to solve concrete, open problems regarding survival and reproduction; the theoretical mind is merely a side-effect of functioning in an environment that requires creativity. This turbulent environment is mainly one's own social group, which provides individuals with great possibilities, but also the challenges of changeability, unpredictability and creativity. In the great, interesting research on human cognitive processes that are determined by evolution, one can point to syndromes of fast learning based on aversive experience and biological bases for conditioning, and the specific character of learning in the processes of primary and secondary socialisation[106].

6. Group and organisational bonds: kin and non-kin altruism

Explaining the creation of group bonds, especially kin bonds, became one of the first problems in the modern application of evolutionism to the social sciences. According to research by W.D. Hamilton, O. Williams and R.L. Trivers, the reason for the development of kin bonds is genetic community. This also means that the strength of a kin bond is directly proportional to genetic proximity. In the social sciences, this is an important explanation, not only from the point of view of the sociology of the family, but also for the question of nepotism in society. More problematic is the interpretation of non-kin altruism. Why are individuals willing to share with other, genetically unrelated individuals? An explanation to this issue is provided by experiments from research in evolutionary psychology and ethology. Vampire bats willingly share blood they have gathered with unrelated individuals, in order to save their companions from inevitable death by starvation. They do this because of the law of reciprocity[107]. Other members of the social group expect reciprocity from individuals that have received help. Social species have also been equipped with developed mental modules, which serve to identify and punish social frauds, who are reluctant to return favours.

---

106 M.E.P. Seligman, J.L. Hager, 'Biological Boundaries of Learning: The Sauce-Bernaise Syndrome', in: *The Functional Mind. Readings in Evolutionary Psychology,* D.T. Kenrick, CL. Luce (eds.), Pearson, Boston, 2004.

107 R. Axelrod, *The Evolution of Cooperation,* Basic Books, New York, 1984.

In management, it is crucial to study social bonds thoroughly because they are reflected in organisational bonds. Nepotism is a culturally universal mechanism, which can manifest itself in the development of family businesses but also in creation of family cliques in companies and public organisations. Non-kin altruism also occurs in organisations and is the basis for human cooperation.

The mechanisms of identification and punishment of social frauds form a basis for social games in every type of organisation. Reference to the evolutionary interpretation of social bonds is therefore crucial for proper modelling of organisational processes.

7. Risk-taking in a social group

A tendency to take risks seems somewhat paradoxical from the evolutionary perspective, however only with regards to the survival of individuals. When interpreted from the point of view of reproduction, evolutionary motives become coherent. Taking risks, especially by males, is a method for strengthening the reproduction success, mainly for individuals with non-dominant positions. When the alpha male achieves greatest reproduction effects, the determination of other males to take risks increases. In the case of social species, such as humans or apes, the risk does not have to be related solely to a physical, individual confrontation; it can involve the formation of a coalition. In the case of humans, this is related to the possibility of a symbolic confrontation, i.e. one that manifests domination in the area that is key from the social point of view[108]. Risk-taking often has a demonstrative aspect, which involves the manifestation of domination and discourages confrontation in the case of sexual competition or attack[109].

A tendency to take risks in management is one of the most crucial features of dynamics in the world of organisations. Entrepreneurship is the readiness to take risks in the development of a new undertaking. Financial and life risks are inseparable in the actions of a manager and entrepreneur. It is interesting how deeply rooted in human nature is the tendency to take risks.

---

108 M. Wilson, M. Daly, 'Competitiveness, Risk Taking, and Violence: The Young Male Syndrome', in: *The Functional Mind. Readings in Evolutionary Psychology,* D.T. Kenrick, CL. Luce (eds.), Pearson, Boston, 2004.

109 J. Dimond, *The Third Chimpanzee. The Evolution and the Future of the Human Animal,* Harper, New York, 1992, pp. 192–215.

8. Group and organisational communication

One condition for permanent change and development in a human community is accumulation of knowledge and achievements. On a larger scale, this is possible thanks to the processes of communication. The beginnings of these processes can be observed in birds and mammals, especially apes; however, language that is able to transfer complex and abstract ideas is probably exclusive to the human species and originates from the coupling of social development and brain specialisation. The author of the nativist concept of language, which is currently developed by evolutionary psychology[110], was Noam Chomsky[111]. Human ability to learn and use a language presumably evolved from a simple system of audible signals, which subsequently served as a means to express emotions and ideas, and describe reality. Next to the system of verbal communication, there developed, probably slightly earlier, a module for quick non-verbal communication, including facial expressions and gestures[112].

Language, which is a sophisticated symbolic system, provided an important stimulus for integration in social groups, and change and formation of more developed groups and societies. Due to the lack of material evidence about the development of speech, it is very difficult to analyse the evolutionary influence of language development on the human species; language, however, might have been one of the causes of the great shift, which led to the creation of *Homo sapiens* in their current form[113]. Language is the key binding element of every social group and organisation, and a basis for the creation of culture. It is often taken for granted, which is why in the management sciences its role was not noticed until it was seen in relation to comparative intercultural studies[114].

---

110 S. Pinker, 'Language as an Adaptation on the Cognitive Niche', in: *The Functional Mind. Readings in Evolutionary Psychology,* D.T. Kenrick, CL. Luce (eds.), Pearson, Boston, 2004.

111 N. Chomsky, *Language and Thought*, Mayer Bell, Wakefield, Rhode Island, London, 1993.

112 P. Ekman, W.V. Friesen, 'Constants across Cultures in the Face and Emotion', in: *The Functional Mind. Readings in Evolutionary Psychology,* D.T. Kenrick, C.L. Luce (eds.), Pearson, Boston, 2004.

113 J. Dimond, *The Third Chimpanzee. The Evolution and the Future of the Human Animal*, Harper, New York, 1992, pp. 141–167.

114 cf. G. Hofstede, *Culture's Consequences: International Differences in Work-Related Values,* Sage Publications, Beverly Hills, 1980.

9. Masculinity and femininity

Evolutionary psychology has clearly proved that cognitive and emotional systems differ in men and women, as a result of evolution. Motoric differentiation, which results directly from physiological and hormonal differences, is obvious. The most important cognitive differences, however, are related to spatial orientation[115] and mathematical and linguistic skills. Emotional differences, on the other hand, refer to distinctions in the accepted, general 'theories of the mind'[116]. In social sciences based on the culturalist vision, the dogma of political correctness that eliminated differences between men and women that had a biological basis was popular. However, empirical research in evolutionary psychology has shown that such differences, which although not fundamental, can be crucial to certain aspects of social functioning. This is why the management sciences should probably consider organisation in terms of relations between the sexes, and analyse the process of management and organisation that takes into account the differing preferences of men and women.

10. Evolutionary conditions for the culture of societies and organisations

Culture can be understood as a symbolic system that comprises a set of beliefs, norms and models, which are transferred between individuals of a social group. The cultural carrier is a common language, and cultural transfer enables the accumulation of knowledge and the achievements of a society. Some evolutionary questions regarding culture still remain valid, namely whether it is adaptation that increases the chances of survival for individuals, an intermediate product of the development of other evolutionary structures (e.g. language and communication), or a by-product, some of whose effects can be harmful to the survival of individuals. An evolutionary theory of culture has not yet been formulated. There are some hypotheses, including memetics[117], which point to analogies between biological evolution and

---

115 M. Eals, I. Silverman, 'The Hunter-Gatherer Theory of Spatial Sex Differences: Proximate Factors Mediating the Female Advantage in Recall of Object Arrays', in: *The Functional Mind. Readings in Evolutionary Psychology,* D.T. Kenrick, C.L. Luce (eds.), Pearson, Boston, 2004.

116 M.G. Haselton, D.M. Buss, 'Error Management Theory: A New Perspective on Biases in Cross-Sex Mind Reading', in: *The Functional Mind. Readings in Evolutionary Psychology,* D.T. Kenrick, C.L. Luce (eds.), Pearson, Boston, 2004.

117 R. Dawkins, *The Selfish Gene*, Oxford University Press, Oxford, 1976.

cultural change[118], but so far they are just concepts in the early stages of formulation or testing.

Basic research conducted in neuroscience gives hope for finding fundamental brain mechanisms that reflect cognitive processes related to the creation of the phenomenon of culture[119]. According to Michael Tomasello, the human cognitive system is based on the cultural fundament, which enables the accumulation of achievements, the identification of individuals with the community, learning, communication, and the development of abstract thinking and creativity[120]. In the social sciences, culture is a key concept. It is core to sociology, cultural anthropology, social psychology, history and other disciplines. The concept of organisational culture in the management sciences derives from the interpretation of culture in the humanist sciences. Explanation of the biological mechanisms of cultural transmission will probably be a crucial achievement for all disciplines that use the theory of culture. In addition, it will indubitably contribute to a better understanding of the complexity of organisational culture and related concepts, such as organisational identity or image.

Evolutionary explanations of social processes are not just hypotheses, but constitute theories that have been verified by empirical research which agree with the basic assumptions of the neoevolutionary paradigm. Research methodology used in evolutionary psychology, sociobiology and neuroscience uses both traditional tools from the social sciences, such as survey research, comparative research, observation and quantitative techniques, and techniques for the examination of the brain (e.g. PET) and animal behaviours, which previously were only used in the natural sciences.

Table 3 shows an attempt at the interpretation of the relationship between the evolutionary nature of man and the resulting nature of a social group, which leads to the description of the organisational process. It does not include all elements of the theory of evolutionary psychology, since research on some aspects of human behaviour in the context of management is very limited.

---

118 R. Allott, 'Evolution and Culture: The Missing Link', in: *The Darwinian Heritage and Sociobiology,* J.G. Dennen, D. Smillie, D.R. Wilson (eds.), Praeger, Westport CT, 1999, pp. 67-70.

119 B.E. Wexler, *Neurobiology, Ideology and Social Change,* A Bradford Book, MIT Press, Cambridge Mass., 2006.

120 M. Tomasello, *Kulturowe źródła ludzkiego poznania,* PIW, Warsaw, 2002, pp. 18-19.

Table 3. The nature of an individual and a social and organisation process in light of the neoevolutionary paradigm.

Nature of an individual	Nature of a social group	Organisational process
1	2	3
Social nature of an individual	Spontaneous emergence of a social group: communication, power, structure and bonds	Spontaneous emergence of organisational processes: leadership, plan, motivation
Kin altruism	Strong kin bonds, the core of a group constituted by coalitions of relatives; Parental investment	Culturally universal influence of nepotism on organisation
Mutual cooperation with the unrelated	Alliances and coalitions between the unrelated, leading to mutual benefit	Creation of an organisation understood as a social group pursuing the realisation of a joint project
Natural sources of the structure of power and hierarchy	Spontaneous emergence of power, structure and hierarchy that puts the social group in order	Informal, and then formal structure, hierarchy and power are intuitively understood and accepted as a natural order
Pursuit of domination, fight and conflict	Fight for domination and conflict are an immanent feature of a social group and intergroup relations (e.g. war)	Pursuit of domination, fight and conflict are a source of intraorganisational competition and a driving force behind rivalry between organisations
Sexual selection	Drive to reproduce and selection of sexual partners with the greatest possible evolutionary value	Disguised importance of sexual motivation in rivalry between individuals in organisations
Leadership, exercising power	A leader or coalition of leaders emerge naturally and pursue the consolidation of power	Leaders are recognised, they gain or lose authority and legitimisation, and can make decisions on behalf of their group
Learning, innovativeness, resourcefulness, creativity	Solving open problems in a changeable environment (also social environment) requires creativity, which is rewarded in a group	The symptom of creativity and innovativeness in an organisation is entrepreneurship, which combines intellectual potential and organisational activities

Cognitive processes – selective memory (people, faces, narration)	Adaptation to act and organise in a small group, in which contacts between individuals are of a personal character	Results: limited range of management, greater entrepreneurship of small groups and bureaucratic tendencies of large organisations
Planning for the future	Social decisions and group's survival strategies that take the future into account	The process of informal and formal planning of versions in group actions and control over their implementation
Group and organisational communication	Language community brings: bond strengthening and possibilities for accumulation and transfer of group knowledge	Communication is a key aspect of organisation, leadership and management, from the point of view of organisational identity as well as process coordination
Evolutionary conditions of culture	Spontaneous emergence of culture based on communication community in a group	Spontaneous emergence of organisational cultures and management cultural models

Source: Own work.

Examples of the use of neoevolutionary inspirations in management

Human nature, whose evolutionary roots grew from the past of the human species and the species by which it was preceded, is reflected through man's actions in many areas of organisational life which are the subject of interest of the management sciences. These include human resource management, organisational behaviours, the sociology of organisations and the theory of organisation and marketing.

The theory of organisation, which is based on evolutionary assumptions, includes the structure of needs and the evolutionary construction of man's cognitive and emotional system. This means, among other things, the assumption that in all motives for action one should look for a hidden meaning in the form of the strengthening of individual's position and physical or symbolic reproduction. Modern society, groups and organisations are perceived through the prism of millions of years of experience of primates in hunter-gatherer groups. Man's needs, fears, phobias, beliefs, stereotypes, metaphors and emotions are therefore rooted in that time and space. Although nowadays people have access to state-of-the-art technologies and the most abstract knowledge, emotionally they remain on the same level as troglodytes.

The search for evolutionary inspirations for the development of organisational structures refers to the notions of power and hierarchy. Paths for spontaneous development of organisational processes and self-organisation, and the formation of power and authority, may be sought. The influence of evolutionary conditions on the creation of formalised structures, at the current stage of cognition, seems difficult to specify clearly. Power and hierarchy, however, are fundamental actions that are deeply rooted in the human mind and based on biological fundaments.

The strategy of organisation, on the other hand, refers to the concept of planning and game. With the development of mental skills, the human species has gained the possibility to plan the future, and computational skills to play multivariate games that enable the calculation of profits and choice of optimal solutions. Strategies chosen by leaders or collectively affect the entire community; there are, therefore, deep and often unconscious decision-making mechanisms. One such poorly-studied mechanism that plays a significant role in management is making decisions in accordance with one's intuition. According to Antonio Damasio, a symptom of intuitive decision-making is the somatic and emotional reaction of the organism, e.g. uncertainty related to a variant that is excessively risky is manifested by fear and stomach cramps[121]. Many authors suggest that most decisions are made unconsciously, in an instant, and our conscious interpretations are only post-factum rationalisations[122].

Management processes are related to the fight for domination in a group and abilities to create coalitions and communicate. It is an interesting challenge to search for psychological and social profiles of alpha individuals, leaders and coalition leaders, and to describe the dynamics of their interplay with the group. After all, leadership is a dynamic process, related to the team profile and their tasks' character; simultaneously, it is inherently bound to a leader's characteristic features and his relations with the group. Distinction between 'male' and 'female' management styles can result from differences in the structure of the cognitive and emotional systems.

Human resource management uses theories of recruitment, motivation and development that are based on an overly-rationalised vision of human nature, which is close to the assumptions of *Homo economicus*. However, as brain research shows, many decision-making processes are beyond the control of

121 A.R. Damasio, *Descartes' Error: Emotion, Reason, and the Human Brain*, Putnam, New York, 1994.

122 cf. K.E. Weick, *Managing the Unexpected,* Jossey-Bass, San Francisco, 2001; M. Gladwell, *Blink: The Power of Thinking Without Thinking,* Time Warner Book Group, New York, 2005.

consciousness, which requires a revision of the human resource management theory[123].

Marketing and organisational behaviours are conditioned, both in theory and practice, by evolutionary heritage related to such issues as the selection of partners, and the valuation system that favours behaviours conducive to survival in a primitive group.

Many evolutionary explanations enable a better understanding of psychological and social bases of the effect of money (i.e. risk factors, speculations on the stock exchange, thriftiness, wastefulness etc). Supported by reliable brain examination, Darwinism helps provide knowledge useful in strategic management. Planning, a sense of time and the tendency toward risk-taking have grown on the biological bases of human cognitive and emotional systems, and have increased chances for survival in the conditions of primitive communities.

The above-mentioned examples referred to various problems and subdisciplines. It seems that evolutionary thinking might be an interesting and universal interpretative basis, leading to a deeper understanding of individual behaviours and actions of social groups and organisations.

Summary

Evolutionism opens the management sciences to new horizons. It is possible to reinterpret many organisational and management phenomena from the perspective of the description of human nature rooted in the process of evolution:

1. The theory of organisation should take into account the influence of the human nature and evolutionary characteristics of a social group on the management process.
2. An organisation is also a coalition of individuals who cooperate with one another, and who are connected by social bonds of evolutionary nature.
3. Important organisational motives include: pursuit of the consolidation of power and individual influence, greater status, and pursuit of symbolic reproduction.
4. Strategic, structural and cultural organisational processes are rooted in the evolutionary concepts.

Many subdisciplines, such as human resource management, marketing, strategic management and finance, can use results of the research on the evolutionary

123 S.M. Colarelli, *No Best Way. An Evolutionary Perspective on Human Resource Management,* Praeger, London, 2003.

sources of human behaviour to create models of man's economic and organisational actions.

Neoevolutionism must not be treated as a solution to all cognitive problems of the social sciences. On the contrary, we are unable to answer many questions that emerge with the application of the evolutionary paradigm to human behaviour. For instance, why are people not slaves of genetic reproduction in their behaviour? As a consequence, an epistemological solution seems to be an attempt to combine research results and interpretations from social disciplines with the evolutionary manner of thinking, with research results from the natural sciences, such as biology, genetics, ethology, information technology and neuroscience. I hope that such a combination will make it possible to solve the most complex cognitive problems concerning the world of man, which previously were exclusive to the social and humanist sciences.

Universalism is the basic value in the evolutionary paradigm, newly researched in the social sciences. It can be the basis for the description of human behaviours from various points of view, regardless of affiliation to different disciplinary discourses. Evolutionary inspirations are interdisciplinary; they set new research fields that combine psychology, sociology, anthropology, information technology, cognitivism, neuroscience and biology with the management sciences. Universalism and interdisciplinarity do not attempt to remove detailed disciplines from the scientific discourse. The evolutionary paradigm can serve as a basis for the consideration of many detailed problems, and it seems pointless to assume the reductionist position that limits the description of human behaviour solely to biological interpretations.

Another value of the evolutionary paradigm is the empirical methodology of research, which not only makes it possible to diagnose and describe a state, but also to construct models and forecast changes. The use of the most recent results in the research on the brain and behaviours, sophisticated mathematical apparatus and creative association of interpretations derived from various sciences are conducive to the development of research, previously limited by the methodology of indirect research, on an unprecedented scale. It seems, therefore, that management, similarly to other social sciences, has a chance to more deeply understand the human nature found in many areas of interest of our discipline. The processes of management, leadership and exertion of power, communication, conflict and cooperation, as well as relations and differences between the sexes cannot be explained without reference to evolutionism. The new paradigm, which can be described as neoevolutionism, has combined a lot of research and theories to build a coherent – from the point of view of the social sciences – image of man in the environment.

Chapter 4
The neoevolutionary methodology in the social sciences

Introduction

Neoevolutionism uses a methodology that has its roots in the natural sciences. This means that it focuses on experimental and observational methods, with control of the variables. The model of explanation is of a cause-effect character and in its final stage should assume the form of mathematical formalism. Development of the neoevolutionary methodology in the social sciences was made possible thanks to the development of brain examination techniques, and a synthetic version of the neoevolutionary theory had been created by the 1970s. Radical propositions for uses of the perspective in the social sciences were included in sociobiology. However, due to differing accents on biological determinism and, most of all, weak research in the area and lack of empirical material, these were met with stern criticism in social science circles. It was not until empirical material was collected in the process of the development of new disciplines, namely neuroscience and evolutionary psychology, that the theory of neoevolutionism and its canon of research methodology in the social sciences crystallised.

The social sciences then developed their own methodology, which differs depending on the discipline and cognitive perspective. Specific methods are used, for example, in history, psychology, sociology and economics. Some disciplines of the social sciences, such as management and cultural anthropology, largely adapt methods of other disciplines for their own cognitive objectives. The caesura between quantitative and qualitative methods in the social sciences is also clearly visible: the quantitative methods have their roots in neopositivism and are based on statistical research and postulate representativeness, while the qualitative methods derive from the symbolic-interpretive paradigm (of hermeneutics and phenomenology) and are of an understanding and exploratory character. From the point of view of epistemological ideals, the methods proposed by neoevolutionism are of a quantitative character. It seems, however, that the innovative methodology of neoevolutionism, including the use of most recent technologies in the examination of the brain and human behaviours, can be a source of cognitive revolution in the social sciences. In my opinion, one should not exclude the possibility of the integration of various methods, both quantitative and qualitative, with the methodology of neopositivist research.

The methodology of the social sciences

The methodology of the social sciences facilitates an understanding of the functioning of objects at the highest level of complexity. Regardless of the cognitive perspective, problems of the human psyche, culture, organisation and society are considered most difficult, as far as cognition is concerned. The systemic school indicates the highest level of the organisation, complexity and emergence of mental and social and cultural processes[124], while the symbolic-interpretive paradigm, hermeneutics and phenomenology reject the possibility of reducing the world of 'sense' and 'understanding' to the level of the natural sciences[125]. Most postmodernists are sceptical of the cognition of the mind and culture[126]. However, it seems that research on the mind, culture and society is making progress, within many paradigms and disciplines of science. It is therefore worthwhile to reflect on concrete research problems and possible methods of their analysis.

Examination of the human mind is a subject of various disciplines that belong to the natural or social sciences, or that straddle the line between them. The most important include biology, psychology, neurology, neuroscience, psychiatry, anthropology and sociology. The human psyche can be analysed on the basis of[127]:

1. Functional, physiological and morphological examination of the brain;
2. Clinical, psychological, psychiatric and neurological examination;
3. Medical history and psychoanalytical examination;
4. Research on AI, neural and cell networks (mathematical modelling);
5. Palaeoanthropological research on hominids and anthropoids;

---

124 L. von Bertanlaffy, J.W. Sutherland, *General Systems Theory: Foundations, Developments, Applications*, George Braziller, New York, 1976.

125 C. Geertz, *The Interpretation of Cultures*, Basic, New York, 1973.

126 R. Rorty, *Philosophy and the Mirror of Nature*, Princeton University Press, Princeton, 2009.

127 R.D. Alexander, *The evolution of the human psyche. In The Human Revolution*, C. Stringer, P. Mellars (eds), Univ. of Edinburgh Press, 1989, pp. 455-513.

6. Ethological, behavioural, sociobiological and primatological research, comparing humans to other species[128].

Culture and society can be examined directly by means of all research related to the human mind, but also indirectly, by trying to reach the level of the consciousness of society, culture or other group entities. The research conducted primarily includes:

1. Observation of social and cultural processes;
2. Interrogative research with participants of social situations (surveys and opinion polls)[129];
3. Qualitative research (ethnographic and biographic research, focus groups and in-depth interviews, grounded theory)[130];
4. Social experiments and quasi-experiments[131];
5. Descriptive studies and analysis of historical data;
6. Statistical data analysis[132].

Research on culture and society is a subject of various disciplines of the social sciences, such as sociology, cultural anthropology, economics, cultural studies and linguistics.

Cognitive stages of the theory of evolution

The theory of evolution functions on many cognitive levels. In the most general understanding, it has a character of a paradigm with many assumptions regarding the cognition of reality. These are the assumptions of cognitive monism, realism, objectivism, verificationism or falsificationism, evolutionary cognitivism and universalism. From this epistemological level, the

---

128 K.Z. Lorenz, *The Comparative Method in Studying Innate Behaviour Patterns,* Symposia of the Society for Experimental Biology, no. 4, Cambridge University Press, Cambridge, 1950, pp. 221-268.

129 S. Nowak, *Metodologia badań społecznych,* Wydawnictwo Naukowe PWN, Warsaw, 2007.

130 N.K. Denzin, Y.S. Lincoln, *The Sage Handbook of Qualitative Research,* 3rd ed. Sage Publications, London, 2005

131 J.J. Shaughnessy, E.B. Zechmeister, J.S. Zechmeister, *Research methods in psychology*, 8th edition, 2009, New York: McGraw-Hill.

132 E.R. Babbie, *The Basics of Social Research*, Cengage Learning, 2008.
C. Frankfort-Nachmias, A. Leon-Guerrero, *Social Statistics for a Diverse Society*, Pine Forge Press, 2010.

neoevolutionary methodology has evolved, which formulates rules for the conduct of research. These are largely convergent with the rules that form the basis for other disciplines of the natural sciences. It is postulated that the canon of modern science be used, i.e. the methods of the natural sciences, especially experiment and controlled observation. Research results should be measureable and the acquired data should lead to mathematical modelling. The explanation is of a cause-effect character, with the use of classification of dependent and independent variables. A lower level of generality can serve for a detailed research methodology, which specifies methods for examining social reality, leading to cognitively valuable results on the grounds of the social sciences.

Using equally strict cognitive criteria for the social sciences as for the natural sciences, neoevolutionism constitutes an ambitious cognitive attempt, which to some extent imitates neopositivism, whilst trying to avoid its mistakes. Therefore neoevolutionists do not seek certainty of cognition, and are not enthusiasts of full verificationism and focus on the development of empirical research, whilst rarely dealing with problems of the philosophy of science (Table 4).

Table 4. The levels of neoevolutionary epistemology

Level	**Content**	**Relationships**
Paradigm	Scientific realism Objectivism Reductionism Verificationism, falsificationism General theory of evolution	Basic level, philosophy of science and generalised theory applied to many disciplines of the natural and social sciences
Methodology	Scientific method modelled on the natural sciences Neopositivist	Intermediate level of general rules for research within the paradigm
Method	Social experiments Brain examination Standardised observation Statistical methods	Operational level, proposals of cognitive and pragmatic methods

Source: Own work.

Another research problem is the description of the evolutionary analysis hierarchy. D.M. Buss differentiates four levels, organised according to the generality of hypotheses. The highest level of generality is constituted by the general theory of evolution, which is a component of the neoevolutionary paradigm. Besides the general theory of evolution, the neoevolutionary paradigm includes assumptions concerning valuable knowledge and the methodology of science. The fundaments of the theory are natural selection, the egoism of genes and sexual selection.

The level of mid-range evolutionary theories includes relatively isolated areas of behaviour, examined and interpreted in evolutionary categories. Examples of such mid-range theories include the theory of parental investments proposed by R. Trivers[133], or the theory of mutual altruism, formulated by several authors, including R. Trivers, J. Tooby and L. Cosmides[134]. Mid-range evolutionary theories have a slightly conventional and historical character but can be subject to empirical verification.

The third level of functioning of evolutionary theories is constituted by detailed evolutionary hypotheses that logically result from the higher levels and can be verified or falsified in a specific research programme. For example, D.M. Buss and D. Symons put forward a hypothesis within evolutionary psychology, according to which "women have developed a specific preference in their choice of men for those with bigger resources"[135]. Their justification for the hypothesis is the claim that women invest much more time and effort in their offspring and therefore have to maximise their chance of success more than men. This means that, regardless of culture, women should: 1) highly estimate life resources, i.e. status, and hence also older partners; 2) men with a high social position will be the most attractive to women; 3) women are inclined to divorce men who do not fulfil their economic needs. Another example is the hypothesis about women's preference for men with an athletic build. Physical conditions related to men's symmetrical and athletic builds also constitute a resource. This is related to the evolutionary past of the species, which spent most of its evolutionary period of functioning in hunter-gatherer communities in which physical resources might have been the basis of a man's success as a hunter. In modern times, the attachment to physical attributes has remained[136]. Verification of the hypothesis included representative intercultural research, in which the most important

---

133 R. Trivers, *Social Evolution*, The Benjamin/Cummings Publishing Company, Inc., California, 1985.

134 D.M. Buss, *Evolutionary Psychology. The New Science of the Mind*, Pearson, Boston, 2008, p. 290.

135 D.M. Buss, 'Sex Differences in Human Mate Preferences: Evolutionary Hypotheses Tested in 37 Cultures', *Behav. Brain Sci.*, 1989, no. 12, pp. 1-49; D. Symons, *The Evolution of Human Sexuality,* Oxford University Press, New York, 1979.

136 J. Tooby, I. DeVore, 'The Reconstruction of Hominid Behavioral Evolution through Strategic Modeling', in: *Primate Models of Hominid Behavior,* W. Kinzey (ed.), SUNY Press, New York, 1987.

factors that were sought were related to the choice of life partners by women in various societies[137].

D.M. Buss points out two basic research strategies used in the testing of evolutionary hypotheses. The first has the character of a top-down strategy (based on theory), where hypotheses are extrapolated from the general evolutionary theory and subsequently projections resulting from the hypotheses are tested, which leads to their verification or falsification and, finally, to assessment of whether empirical results confirm the projections resulting from the hypotheses. Such corroboration of hypotheses facilitates the development of the theory on several levels. The second research strategy is more frequently used in evolutionary psychology due to richer empirical data, and is a bottom-up strategy (based on observations). Hypotheses are made on the basis of observations and experiments, after which projections resulting from the hypotheses and assessment of their conformity with empirical research are tested[138]. Both strategies are modelled on methods of the natural sciences, and in an idealised form, take the shape of deduction or scientific induction.

New Research Methods in Social Sciences

In the sphere of methodology, the evolutionary paradigm is orientated to the use of the scientific methods of the natural sciences, especially experiment and controlled observation. Methodological rigors include representativeness and randomisation of trials, and control of variables, which facilitates the presentation of research results in a mathematical form. Experimentation, or alternatively observation, should lead to an incomplete verification or falsification of hypotheses resulting from theory. It seems then that the use of the experimental method in the social sciences requires its adaptation to problems of the highest level of complexity. It also does not seem sensible to reject the methodological achievements gained so far by the social sciences. The methodology of the neoevolutionary trend in the social sciences will therefore be eclectic. Its core will be formed by the methods of social experiment and controlled observation, but it will also be possible to reach, in research programmes, for the quantitative and qualitative methodology of traditionally understood social sciences.

The largest amount of research that can be considered rooted in the neoevolutionary trend has been conducted within evolutionary psychology[139].

137 D.M. Buss, *Evolutionary Psychology*, op. cit., pp. 42-46.

138 ibid., p. 47.

139 Ch. Crawford, D. Krebs, *Foundations of Evolutionary Psychology,* Lawrence Erlbaum Associates, Mahwah, NJ, 2008.

Dominating here are the methods of experiment and quasi-experiment, observation and descriptive methods[140]. Psychology has developed methods of controlled social experiment, which, enriched with elements of experiment from the sciences, may be applied in experimental psychology[141].

The neoevolutionary trend also includes primatological research, related to the analysis of the behaviour of primates. It primarily includes controlled observations in artificial and natural conditions, experiments and quasi-experiments, including use of physiological examination, e.g. of the brain[142]. The results of such research provide answers to questions regarding the stage of development of cognitive and emotive skills, communication skills and social structures among apes. Comparing them with human communities enables us to discover the specificity of human behaviours.

A separate group of research methods is employed in the subject of palaeoanthropology, which specialises in searching for human traces and excavations concerning primitive human communities, hominids and anthropoids. On the one hand, the discipline is related to palaeontology, using sophisticated methods of research and recognition of excavations, and on the other with anthropology, studying modern and past cultures. Palaeoanthropology provides information regarding the structure, organisation and culture of anthropoids, hominids and primitive man, which facilitates tracing cultural changes from the evolutionary past of the human race[143].

The methodology of anthropological research is partly coherent with the neoevolutionary paradigm, however cultural anthropology based on the symbolic-interpretive paradigm does not share the epistemological assumptions of evolutionists. This does not change the fact that valuable research methods can be used regardless of their origin. Anthropology has developed methods of field ethnological observation and methods of comparative intercultural research[144].

Similarly to this is the situation with other methods of the social sciences derived from sociology, economics, management, history, political science and other disciplines. For example, empirical sociology has accumulated rich

140 J.J. Shaughnessy, E.B. Zechmeister, J.S. Zechmeister, *Research methods in psychology*, McGraw-Hill Education, 2011

141 R.J. Gerrig, P.G. Zimbardo, *Psychology and Life*, Allyn & Bacon, 2009.

142 J.M. Setchell, DJ. Curtis, *Field and Laboratory Methods in Primatology: A Practical Guide,* Cambridge University Press, Cambridge, 2003.

143 R.S. Corruccini, R.L. Ciochon, *Integrative Paths to the Past: Paleoanthropological Advances in Honor of F. Clark Howell,* Prentice Hall, Englewood Cliffs, 1994.

144 H.R. Bernard, *Research Methods in Anthropology: Qualitative and Quantitative Approaches,* Rowman, Altamira, 2006.

methodological achievements in the use of survey methods, which can be successfully used in opinion polls in social groups. Simultaneously, humanist sociology proposed a rich spectrum of qualitative methods. These have the character of exploratory and in-depth research, which although not representative, are suitable for preliminary analysis of social processes with a high level of complexity[145]. Both survey and quantitative and qualitative methods may be applied to many social sciences, and could therefore be used in relation to research consistent with the neoevolutionary trend.

Research within the social sciences that can be located in neoevolutionism, or identified as not contradictory to the trend, includes three areas with various levels of engagement of the theory of evolution:

1. Research that uses the theory of evolution as the main point of theoretical reference;
2. Research that marginally uses the theory of evolution;
3. Research not contradicting the theory of evolution for which it is possible to apply interpretations consistent with evolutionism.

It seems intentional that analysis is limited solely to the first two areas, although the third effectively constitutes the most numerous group.

Known research in the social sciences within the neoevolutionary trend includes three programmes: verification of the hypothesis of cultural universalism with evolutionary roots; indication of the perceptive and cognitive illusions related to the structure of the human cognitive system, and examination of the ability to detect evolutionary cheaters, the human moral sense and decision-making processes. For example, research by P. Ekman indicates a culturally universal character of human facial expressions coupled with emotions and largely independent of conscious control[146]. Results of the research are important because they disprove the assumption of radical cultural relativism that is popular in the postmodern approach.

Research programmes conducted over many years by A. Tversky and D. Kahneman have facilitated the description of a series of cognitive limitations on the human mind concerning, for example, the assessment of probability, the search for algorithms in random sequences and other illusions falsifying the

145 N.K. Denzin, Y.S. Lincoln, *The Sage Handbook of Qualitative Research*, 3rd ed., Sage Publications, London, 2005.

146 P. Ekman, W.V. Friesen, 'Constants Across Cultures in the Face and Emotion', in: *The Functional Mind. Readings in Evolutionary Psychology,* D.T. Kenrick, CL. Luce (eds.), Pearson, Boston, 2004.

picture of reality[147]. J. Tooby and L. Cosmides conducted social experiments concerning the adaptation of the human mind to detecting evolutionary cheaters, i.e. individuals that only simulate group cooperation, whilst being in reality untrustworthy[148]. Also famous are the observations and quasi-experiments on chimpanzees conducted by J. Goodall, and later by F. de Waal, indicating that our simian relatives show many traits that used to be considered exclusively human, such as cooperation and formation of coalitions, wars, intrigues, communication, creation and use of tools, and even a moral sense[149].

Neoevolutionary methods in management

In management, archaic social basic theories related to human nature, the mind and society are dominant. For example, we can quote excellent theories of motivation by A. Maslow and F. Herzberg, which are nevertheless inadequate to the modern level of knowledge in psychology and sociology[150]. A significant amount of research indicates the evolutionary origin of the complexity of motivational mechanisms, which can be explained, for example, by the modular structure of the mind[151] or by needs originating from the human environment (competition in a social group).

So far, attempts to apply the neoevolutionary perspective in management studies have been very limited. Evolution itself has been a source of numerous and expressive metaphors describing the development of a market or sector, the life cycle of an organisation, or the changes in organisational culture. However, the use of neoevolutionism in describing human behaviours in the organisational process is slight. From the point of view of management studies, the

147 A. Tversky, D. Kahneman, 'Availability: A Heuristics for Judging Frequency and Probability', in: *Judgment Under Uncertainty: Heuristics and Biases,* D. Kahneman, P. Slovic, A. Tversky (eds.), Cambridge University Press, New York, 1982.

148 J. Tooby, L. Cosmides, 'Toward Mapping the Evolved Functional Organization of Mind and Brain', in: *The New Cognitive Neuroscience,* M.S. Gazzaniga (ed.), MIT Press, Cambridge Mass., 2000.

149 J. Goodall, *Through a Window: My Thirty Years with the Chimpanzees of Gombe*, Houghton Mifflin, Boston, 1990; F. de Waal, *Chimpanzee Politics: Sex and Power among Apes*, The Johns Hopkins University Press, Baltimore, 1982.

150 A.H. Maslow, 'A Theory of Human Motivation', *Psychological Review*, 1943, no. 50(4), pp. 370-396; F. Herzberg, *The Motivation to Work,* John Wiley and Sons, New York, 1959.

151 J. Tooby, L. Cosmides, 'Toward Mapping the Evolved Functional Organization of Mind and Brain', in: *The New Cognitive Neuroscience,* M.S. Gazzaniga (ed.), MIT Press, Cambridge Mass., 2000; J.A. Fodor, *The Modularity of Mind: An Essay in Faculty Psychology,* MIT Press, Cambridge Mass., 1983.

neoevolutionary methodology is important mainly as a source of basic theory. Models of human behaviour related to exertion of power and leadership, creation of social structures, the process of forecasting the future and planning, the creation of culture, cooperation with other people and organisation of work – all facilitate the creation of effective management rules.

It seems, however, that examining the process of organisation and management could also take the form of research programmes using the neoevolutionary methodology. Such research could formulate cognitive objectives in the form of identification of evolutionary, genetic, and also environmental conditions of organisation, management, power and leadership, organisational culture, the process of planning and strategising, and many other aspects of organisation. In such programmes, it would be possible to conduct interdisciplinary research based on methodological pluralism. The spectrum of methods could then include palaeoanthropological and ethnological methods, social experiments and brain examination, comparative intercultural studies (quantitative and qualitative), and primatological studies. Obviously, a research programme should integrate primary and secondary sources of data. Some forms of research are secondary by nature, e.g. palaeoanthropological excavations conducted continuously, and not for individual social studies. It seems that integrated and interdisciplinary programmes can be an opportunity for development for many social sciences, including management studies (Table 5).

Table 5. Suggestions for integrated research programmes involving management studies using the neoevolutionary methodology

Area of management	**Sample research questions**	**Hypotheses**	**Research methodology**
1	**2**	**3**	**4**
Organisation	1. To what extent is organisation genetically conditioned? 1. What is the influence of evolutionary variables on the process of organisation? 2. Does the process of organisation involve genetic-environmental	1. Organisation is a natural feature of human community. 2. Organisation is based on cooperation and competing for resources. 3. Organisation is man's primary need. 4. Organisation is a coupling of unconscious and conscious actions.	1. Ethnological research, comparative studies of primitive communities. 2. Literature and anthropological data on primitive communities. 3. Social experiments using brain examination. 4. Palaeoanthropological excavations of primitive people,

<table>
<tr><td></td><td>coupling. If yes, what does this involve?</td><td></td><td rowspan="5">hominids and anthropoids.
5. Comparative primatological studies (chimpanzees).
6. Quantitative comparative intercultural studies in search of cultural universals (survey method with large representative samples).
7. Qualitative intercultural studies exploring cultural diversity (in-depth interviews, ethnomethodology).
8. Qualitative comparative studies – studies of cases of organisational activities.</td></tr>
<tr><td>Power</td><td>1. What are the sources of power in a social group?
2. Is power genetically conditioned?
3. How flexible is the hierarchy in a human community?</td><td>1. Power stems from the animal pecking order.
2. People have various levels of need for the exertion of power.
3. On average, women have a lower need for power.</td></tr>
<tr><td>Leadership</td><td>1. To what extent does leadership derive from innate or acquired characteristics?
2. How does informal leadership form in a small group?</td><td>1. Leadership skills derive from the innate and acquired characteristics of a leader and from the social characteristics of the group.
2. Leaders in a small group emerge from among those individuals showing Machiavellian intelligence.</td></tr>
<tr><td>Organisation-al culture</td><td>1. Does culture emerge spontaneously in an informal group?
2. How can leaders form the culture of their groups?</td><td>1. The culture of a small group is inherently xenophobic.
2. Organisational culture cannot be managed.</td></tr>
<tr><td>Planning and strategy</td><td>1. Among living creatures, is man the only one who attempts to foresee the future?
2. Are planning skills related to brain features (neuronal level)?</td><td>1. Planning appears only in humans and within a group of people.
2. Strategy is an advanced planning skill.</td></tr>
</table>

Source: Own work.

Summary

The methodology of neoevolutionism has proven its efficiency with valuable research in evolutionary psychology and neuroscience. The research conducted has verified, in a probabilistic sense (without assuming certainty), the use of the general theory of evolution and its many specifications on various cognitive levels. Research programmes conducted gather increasingly rich empirical material that makes it possible to describe the human world being the subject of the social and humanistic sciences. Research results lead to a new image of the human mind, society and culture, which is largely inconsistent with traditional assumptions regarding human subjectivity accepted by the social sciences.

It seems very important to include representatives of the social sciences in scientific research and discussions. This could result in the integration of neoevolutionary methods with other traditional methods of the social sciences. Such integration could take the form of research programmes realised by representatives of various disciplines of science. Thanks to this, complex problems of sociological, psychological, economic and anthropological natures could be studied from various perspectives.

However, the lack of interest from most representatives of the social sciences in the research results in neuroscience, cognitivism, palaeoanthropology, biology and evolutionary psychology is problematic. Some results of the neoevolutionary research are momentous and could revolutionise our perception of the human mind and culture. The isolationism of the representatives of the social and humanistic sciences could result in a strengthening of the tendency to differentiate between "two cultures"[152]. Beside the tendency to isolate representatives of the traditionally understood social sciences in "an ivory tower", there also exists an integration trend, a manifestation of which could be seen to be, for instance, the awarding of the 2002 Noble Prize in Economics to Daniel Kahneman, the most famous behavioural economist.

Therefore it seems that several postulates should be proposed in the methodological sphere, which derive from the rapid development of the neoevolutionary methodology:

1. In the various scientific disciplines related to man, culture and society, an analysis should be made of the cognitive adequacy of the neoevolutionary paradigm and methodology;

---

152 C. P. Snow, *The Two Cultures* (1959; Cambridge: Cambridge Univ. Press, 1993).

2. Representatives of the social sciences, especially sociologists, economists, specialists in management, anthropologists and linguists, should start using the methodology developed by the evolutionary perspective;
3. Research programmes conducted by interdisciplinary teams and facilitating the exploration of human behaviour should be integrated;
4. The neoevolutionary perspective should be included in training programmes for researchers in all scientific and humanist sciences.

Chapter 5
Management and the primates

Introduction

DNA tests have confirmed the hypothesis that people are very closely related to chimpanzees. Only one percent of the genome of *Homo sapiens* is different from the genome of *Pan troglodytes*[153]. Should such a close relationship not also result in similar behaviour[154]?

Management, according to the classical definition by H. Fayol, consists of planning, organising, commanding and controlling[155]. The fact that these activities are characteristic solely of humans has been, since the moment the theory of management was created, so obvious that it has never been questioned. However modern discoveries of evolutionary psychology and primatology suggest that most social skills people possess are of biological origin, thus also organisation and management are natural processes[156]. One could advance a thesis that the ability to organise is the foundation of social life, not only of humans, but also of numerous species of ape[157].

The aim of this chapter is to analyse the basic organisational skills that have developed in our closest relatives – apes, mostly chimpanzees and bonobos – and that have been perfected by *Homo sapiens*. It seems that organisational skills have been developing in the course of the primate evolution. Although the possibility of following the development of organisational processes in our pre-human ancestors (*Australopithecus*, *Homo habilis, Homo erectus*) is very limited, in searching for the biological roots of organisational processes one can still use the rich empirical materials that exist, based on the observation of chimpanzees. Analysis of this will prove the continuity of the development of social skills which are the basis for organisation and management; the reason for pursuing this issue are the surprising results (from the point of view of

---

153 K.S. Pollard, "What Makes Us Human?", *Scientific American*, May 2009, pp. 44-49.

154 B. Silk, "Empathy, Sympathy and Prosocial Preferences in Primates", in: R.I.M. Dunbar, L. Barrett, *Evolutionary Psychology*, Oxford University Press, New York, 2007.

155 H. Fayol, *General and Industrial Management,* Pitman, New York, 1949.

156 Ł. Sułkowski, "Paradygmat neoewolucyjny w naukach o zarządzaniu", *Przegląd Organizacji*, vol. 3, 2009.

157 C.P. van Schaik, "Culture in Primate and other Animals", in: R.I.M. Dunbar, L. Barrett, *Evolutionary Psychology,* Oxford University Press, New York 2007.

culturalism's assumptions, rooted in the social sciences), of research into ape behaviour[158].

Cooperation between primates

Cooperation between animals with the aim of increasing the probability of genetic reproduction and their chances for survival in the wild are not uncommon. There are numerous known social species, e.g. insects living in hives, anthills or termite mounds, fish moving in shoals or mammals forming herds. Social species also include our closest biological relatives, i.e. chimpanzees and bonobos[159]. Cooperation amongst chimpanzees is very different from the rigid and simple cooperation patterns characteristic of insects – the many years of observations by primatologists indicate openness, flexibility and even creativity in terms of cooperation patterns. The research carried out by J. Goodall and F. De Waal proves that chimpanzees use a variety of skills in organisational cooperation in order to positively transform their physical surroundings, such as group work, forming teams and groups in order to attack or defend in a collective manner, group imitation of innovative behaviour aimed at survival, group distribution of goods, and the beginnings of hunting specialisations based on sex and age[160].

The basis for cooperation in groups of chimpanzees, hominids and humans is kin and non-kin altruism. Kin altruism means selfless help for one's kin and can be easily explained by the urge to maximise the reproduction of one's genes[161]. Non-kin altruism causes more problems, as it cannot be explained by either simple "gene selfishness" or the group selection suggested by biology[162]. As the research into chimpanzees shows, altruistic behaviour towards members of one's own group is common and profitable. Good examples of non-kin altruism that benefit individuals in the long run are: distribution of limited food resources in accordance with hierarchy, but taking into consideration the needs of weaker individuals, protection against the attacks of rival groups, and mutual searching for fleas. F. De Waal, based on rich empirical materials, even proves

158 S. Pinker, *The Blank Slate: The Modern Denial of Human Nature*, Penguin, 2003.

159 J. Goodall, *In the Shadow of Man*, Houghton Mifflin Harcourt, 2000.

160 F. de Waal, A. van Roosraalen, "Reconciliation and Consolation among Chimpanzees", *Behavioral Ecology and Sociobiology* 1997, no. 5, pp. 55-66.

161 R.L. Trivers, "The Evolution of Reciprocal Altruism", *Quarterly Review of Biology* 1971, no. 46, pp. 35-57.

162 R.L. Trivers, "Evolutionary Biologist", *Social Evolution*, Benjamin-Cummings Publishing Co. 1985.

that not only altruism, but also morality has deep evolutionary roots that can be observed in chimpanzees[163].

Organisational skills are part of the social sphere, and many researchers believe this to be the most important driving force behind the quick evolutionary changes that lead from apes to humans[164]. Among the hypotheses concerning the mechanisms of brain evolution, importance is given to the concept of Machiavellian intelligence, which indicates that selective pressure in a group of hominids favours individuals of above-average intelligence, who strive for control of the others in their group[165].

Another hypothesis – which does not exclude the previous one – concerns the development of cooperation, altruism and social intelligence through the evaluation of hunting communities. Certain hierarchies, distribution of work between the sexes and constant improvement of hunting techniques, would lead to the development of brain, communication and social skills[166]. R Dunbar describes the complexity of social relations in a group of primates, which requires an effective analysis of relations and the choosing of proper responses to different individuals and groups[167]. An increasing degree of socialisation requires higher and higher intelligence in coping with others and, in consequence, differences in intelligence level translate into much greater differences in skill levels, thanks to which individuals are able to manipulate the social structure to their advantage. The key element of Machiavellian intelligence could be the organisational skills which relate, on the one hand, to effective communication within a group, and on the other, to the ability to influence others and gain respect.

Social conflicts in primates societies

In the case of primates, conflicts within groups are significantly different from the conflicts between groups. Internal conflicts are usually short-lived and do

---

163 F. de Waal, *Primates and Philosophers. How Morality Evolved*, Princeton University Press, Princeton, Oxford 2006.

164 N.K. Humphrey, "The Social Function of Intelect" in: *Growing points in Ethology*, P.P.G. Baetson, R.A. Hinde (eds.), Cambridge University Press, Cambridge 1976.

165 A. Whiten, R.W. Byrne (eds.), *Machiavellian Intelligence II: Extensions and Evaluations*, Cambridge University Press, Cambridge 1997.

166 N.V. Watson, "Sex Differences in Throwing. Monkeys having a Fling", *Trends in Cognitive Science,* 2001, no. 5, pp. 98-99.

167 R.I.M. Dunbar, "Neocortex Size as a Constraint on Group Size in Primates", *Journal of Human Evolution* 1992, no. 20, pp. 469-493.

not pose a threat to the whole group, while conflicts with other groups may take the form of a war, with one group trying to destroy the males of the other.

In a troop of chimpanzees, there are frequent conflicts between individuals, families and coalitions. The underlying causes of conflict are, most of all, food and the possibility of reproducing. Some researchers believe that the conflicts for resources are the biological beginnings of the human possessive instinct[168]. Usually, the feuding parties reconcile by performing social rituals, such as searching for fleas. Often, the intervention of individuals who occupy a higher position in the social hierarchy can also lead to a resolution of the conflict. Sometimes, more serious conflicts result in a division of the troop. However, this only happens in large groups.

Hierarchy and power are clearly visible in the case of most social animals. Conflict over the position of the dominant (alpha) male is inherent in the nature of social structures, and the dominant male – as research shows – is most often an individual who has social and emotional intelligence (ability to form alliances). The dominant male holds the function of group leader, has access to the greatest amount of resources, distributes the goods, intervenes in order to restore social order and takes active part in conflicts with other groups. It seems that the leadership we deal with in the case of humans is based on the biological basis of the alpha male position, and this may also be the source of the irresistible charm of authority over other people, which both politicians and managers know very well.

J. Goodall, who spent many years carrying out research into chimpanzees in the Gombe National Park, was surprised by the violence of the conflicts between the different troops. These took the form of wars, in which gangs of males of one group launched numerous attacks on individuals from another group and killed them. Furthermore, the way the attacks were organised suggested deliberate or even planned actions[169]. One of the hypotheses concerning hominids emphasises the importance of group conflicts, violence and wars for the development of the brain and society of pre-humans. Undoubtedly, conflicts between groups were a mechanism of developing skills related to planning and organisation, and created favourable conditions for the development of communication within a group.

---

168 H. Dittmar, *The Social Psychology of Material Possessions: to Have Is to Be*, Hempel Hempstead, Harvester Wheatsheaf 1992.

169 J. Goodall, *In the Shadow of Man*, Houghton Mifflin Harcourt, 2000.

Organisational abilities of chimpanzees

A comparison of the social skills of humans and chimpanzees leads to the obvious conclusion that *Homo sapiens*, despite considerable genetic similarity to *Pan troglodytes*, possesses significant differences in terms of behaviour. However, such a trivial conclusion should not veil the facts which prove the deep biological and evolutionary roots of human behaviour, including organisational behaviour (Table 6).

Some of the features common to both people and chimpanzees in the field of organisational behaviour include:

1. Teamwork based on cooperation,
2. Combining cooperation with rivalry in order to achieve a certain status,
3. Accepting hierarchy, power, authority and leadership,
4. The ability to think forward, as well as to act in a purposeful and deliberate way,
5. The presence of a system allowing communication of one's emotions and perceived threats,
6. Imitating innovation[170],
7. The origins of culture[171].

Among the features in the organisational sphere unique to people are skills responsible for long-term planning, self-reflection, creation of culture and complex organisational structures, symbolic and abstract thinking, and value-oriented goals. One reason for such great variety of behaviour in the case of genetically similar species could be the rapid and significant development of the cerebral cortex, which is the basis of higher mental functions.

170 M. Tomasello, *The Cultural Origins of Human Cognition*, Harvard University Press, Cambridge Mass 1999, p. 278.

171 L. Rodseth, S. Novak, "The Impact of Primatology on the Study of Human Society" in: *Missing the Revolution. Darwinism for Social Scientists*, J. Barkow (ed.), Oxford University Press, Oxford 2006.

Table 6. Similarities and differences between people and chimpanzees in terms of organisational behaviour.

Organisational behaviour	**Features common to both people and chimpanzees**	**Features distinguishing people from chimpanzees**
Teamwork	Undertaking of common activities related to internal and external conflicts, forming alliances, cooperation while hunting etc.	Formalised organisation and teams that can: define goals, make long-term plans and exercise self-control.
Cooperation	Cooperation between individuals enhanced emotionally, based on similarities, common interests and altruism.	Cooperation in numerous social groups in order to perform diverse and complex tasks.
Rivalry	Based on the need to gain access to as much food and sexual resources as possible.	The ability to create a hierarchy of needs, and thus the degree of rivalry for resources, in a reflective and intuitive way.
Power and hierarchy	Intuitive maintenance of hierarchical order and the impulse to improve one's own status.	Complex social and organisational structures.
Leadership	Leadership based on forming social coalitions that help to maintain authority and power.	Leadership as formalised management. Transformational leadership.
Communication and language	A system of communicating simple emotions and indicating external threats.	Symbolic, abstract and normative spheres of language and culture.
Deliberate and intentional actions	Short-term deliberate and intentional actions.	Self-reflective decision-making. Controlling individual and group decisions.
Planning	Short-term, incidental, informal planning. Trying to limit the degree of uncertainty.	Long-term, systematic planning based on strategic goals and values. Self-awareness of planning and control of plan implementation.

Source: Own work.

Summary

What are the conclusions from the deliberations presented in this chapter? Treating it ironically, not that we should civilise apes. The results of teaching chimpanzees a language have been really poor so far. Instead, we should try to change the way we view ourselves, *Homo sapiens*. Looking for variables that explain our behaviour we can not only use the repertoire of rational actions; we need to refer to the evolutionary heritage that has shaped our minds and significantly influences today's decisions and actions of people.

A comparative analysis based on primatological research has revealed that organisation is also a kind of instinct that we have inherited from our simian ancestors[172]. This is why it seems that in conducting research in organisational behaviour, organisational culture, leadership, cooperation and rivalry in organisations, as well as other related issues, one should also analyse their evolutionary origins and instinctive character. The organisational behaviour and skills of people are shaped by a biological potential linked with environmental conditions, so people are to a certain degree natural organisers. This means that many kinds of organisational behaviour are based on intuition and, although they can be improved by reflection, they are not subject to full rational control.

172 R. Bshary, L.H. Salwiczek, W. Wickler, "Social Cognition in Non-Primates" in: R.I.M. Dunbar, L. Barrett, *Evolutionary Psychology*, Oxford University Press, New York 2007.

Chapter 6
Culture as seen by evolutionists

Introduction

Culture is a notion that is the foundation and, at the same time, the curse of social sciences and humanities. Its ambiguity as a notion makes it extremely difficult to employ. Today, one promising current of research in cultural processes seems to be the neoevolutionary perspective, initiated by sociobiology and creatively developed by evolutionary psychology.

Modern paleontological research is revealing the remains of the culture of hominids and our ancestors, but it hasn't solved the mystery of our cultural origins. From the perspective of evolution, mankind is young, and from the perspective of genetics, it is 99% identical with chimpanzees [173]. The development of evolutionary psychology, cognitive psychology and neuroscience allows for new interpretations of cultural processes that are perceived by analogy with biological evolution. In this sense, the neoevolutionary paradigm is not only included in the famous classification by A.L. Kroeber and C. Kluckhohn, but also introduces new threads into the discussion about the genesis and essence of culture[174].

The aim of this chapter is to review the most important ways of analysing culture from the neoevolutionary perspective. First, the main assumptions of the current thinking are outlined with reference to culture, culture is then defined, and then two different perspectives of cultural analysis are proposed in relation to the neoevolutionary paradigm. The new perspective, originating from primatology, is the analysis of animal protocultures as the basis for the development of *Homo Sapiens* culture[175]. The other perspective is memetics, i.e. the attempt to build a framework of a general replication theory that, by analogy with genetic reproduction, would describe the idea and method of information

---

173 J. Call, "Social Knowledge in Primates" in: R.I.M. Dunbar, L. Barrett, *Evolutionary Psychology*, Oxford University Press, New York 2007.

174 A.L. Kroeber, C. Kluckhohn, *Culture: A Critical Review of Concepts and Definitions*, Wayne Untereiner, Alfred G. Meyer, Peabody Museum 1952.

175 C.P. van Schaik, "Culture in Primate and other Animals" in: R.I.M. Dunbar, L. Barrett, *Evolutionary Psychology*, Oxford University Press, New York 2007.

replication in a cultural environment[176]. The chapter ends with critical remarks concerning the evolutionary aspects of culture.

Neoevolutionary paradigm of culture?

According to S. Pinker, the social sciences of the second half of the 20th century were dominated by the perspective of culturalism, drawing from both the functionalist and interpretative paradigm. To put it very simply, it could be said that culturalism made the following assumptions: *tabula rasa*, cultural relativism and autonomisation of the world of symbols, values and abstraction. S. Pinker criticises the approach popularised by cultural research, drawing from Locke's idea of *tabula rasa*, which means a blank slate and assumes that there is no human nature originating from biological affiliation. *Tabula rasa* means full flexibility of a human mind, thanks to which, through socialisation, one can implement any value, norm and cultural pattern[177].

On the other hand, cultural relativism rejects cultural universals, i.e. elements common to all human cultures, as a consequence of human nature. The assumption that the world of symbols, values and abstraction is autonomous means that these areas are characteristic only of people and that they define the essence of humanity. Language, abstract thinking and morality have developed in the human world and so are alien to natural sciences, thus they should be studied only with the use of methods characteristic of symbolic and axiological reality. This view also coincides with the theological position of most major religions. Thus, the ontological observation about mankind leads to postulates of epistemological nature, concerning cognition, and of pragmatic nature, concerning acting.

The neoevolutionary approach to culture, although as internally diverse as the cultural one, is in clear opposition to the above-mentioned assumptions. S. Pinker points to constant elements of human nature as being a result of our biological heritage. These concern the behavioural sphere, as well as the emotional and mental ones. Thanks to the cerebral 'software' gained through evolution, people learn, use languages, create, understand music, and have a moral and religious sense. But they also get addicted, fight with each other and strive for power[178].

---

176 R. Aunger, "Memes" in: R.I.M. Dunbar, L. Barrett, *Evolutionary Psychology*, Oxford University Press, New York 2007.

177 S. Pinker, The Blank Slate: The Modern Denial of Human Nature, Viking Press, 2002.

178 J.A. Bulbulia, "The Evolution of Religion" in: R.I.M. Dunbar, L. Barrett, *Evolutionary Psychology*, Oxford University Press, New York 2007; J. Carroll, "Evolutionary Ap-

Modern anthropological and psychological research unambiguously indicates that there are cultural universals. Comparative intercultural research into grimaces and facial expressions[179], the moral sense, aesthetics and logic leaves no doubt that although culture diversifies people to a certain extent, there is a great number of physical, mental and emotional features common to all of mankind[180]. Empirical knowledge deals a final blow to the radical cultural relativism, the foundation of which was the development of the postmodernist orientation in the humanities in the 20th century. The discussion covers a full list of universals, however, there is a wide range of features that appear in all human cultures.

For example, D. E. Brown found over 500 cultural universals that have been examined by ethnographers, sociologists and psychologists[181]. These include categories of different reality aspects, from the most general and abstract (planning, culture, language), through detailed abstract categories (economic inequality, succession, nepotism, taboo, myths), to material and symbolic artefacts (toys, tools, nouns).

The neoevolutionary current also rejects the autonomisation of the world of symbols, values and abstraction, referring mostly to analyses of animal protocultures and indicating the continuity in the mental development of species between apes and humans[182]. Extensive empirical materials show that despite the fact that certain aspects of culture are highly developed in human society, they are strongly rooted in animal protocultures. This concerns both social and cognitive skills, and the moral and aesthetic sense. For evolutionists, the consequence of adopting the naturalist position is the epistemological and methodological postulate related to applying scientific methods taken from natural sciences to research into the cultural sphere.

---

proaches to Literature and Drama" in: R.I.M. Dunbar, L. Barrett, *Evolutionary Psychology*, Oxford University Press, New York 2007; I. Cross, "Music and Cognitive Evolution" in: R.I.M. Dunbar, L. Barrett, *Evolutionary Psychology*, Oxford University Press, New York 2007; S. Kirby, "The Evolution of Language" in: R.I.M. Dunbar, L. Barrett, *Evolutionary Psychology*, Oxford University Press, New York 2007.

179 P. Ekman, W.V. Friesen, "Constants across Cultures in the Face and Emotion" in: *The Functional Mind. Readings in Evolutionary Psychology*, D.T. Kensrick, C.L. Luce (eds.), Pearson, Boston 2004.

180 J. Panksepp, "The Neuroevolutionary and Neuroaffective Psychobiology of the Prosocial Brain" in: R.I.M. Dunbar, L. Barrett, *Evolutionary Psychology*, Oxford University Press, New York 2007.

181 D.E. Brown, *Human Universals*, McGraw-Hill, New York 1991.

182 *The Question of Animal Culture*, K. N. Laland, B. G. Galef (eds.), Harvard University Press, Cambridge Mass. 2009; J. Diamond, *The Third Chimpanzee. The Evolution and the Future of the Human Animal*, Harper, New York 1992.

D. C. Dennett, in criticism of the classical statement by C. Geertz that says culture is a web of meanings spun by men that cannot be examined with the use of experimental methods, as they are of an interpretative nature, states: "The fact that we, men, spin a web of meanings is doubtless, but the webs can be analysed with the use of the scientific methods of natural sciences"[183]. The research into cultures set in the neoevolutionary paradigm makes use of traditional observational, questionnaire and statistical methods developed by social sciences, and also introduces experiments examining the responses of people in controlled conditions with the use of magnetic resonance, positron emission and electroencephalography (MRI, PET). A very important role is also played by the research into the origins of cultures and civilisations carried out by palaeoanthropology. The aim of this research lies not only in cultural studies, but also in looking for generalisations, mathematical modelling and predictions, and also in the area of cultural processes. Most evolutionist researchers are aware of the fact that this is an early stage of the development of a new approach to understanding culture, and the first results are very promising.

The essence of culture as seen from the evolutionary perspective

A number of evolutionists' research projects are concerned with culture, which means that there is a significant number of definitions of 'culture', referring to different ways of understanding this phenomenon. Some refer to neurobiological processes[184], others to culture as understood in cognitive terms[185]. C. J. Lumsden and E. O. Wilson[186] believe that cultural transmission takes the form of a link between genes and culture (coevolution), and that the key to explaining culture is in building a theory of information replication covering three levels: genes, mind and culture. A similar view is presented by R. Dawkins, S. Blackmore, D. C. Dennett, L. L. Cavalli-Sforza and M. W. Feldman, trying to create a mathematical theory of the "meme" or "culturgene"[187]. In most meanings of

183 D. Dennett, *Breaking the Spell: Religion as a Natural Phenomenon,* Penguin Group, 2006.; C. Geertz, *The Interpretation of Cultures*, Basic, New York 1973.

184 B.E. Wexler, *Brain and Culture. Neurobiology, Ideology and Social Change*, A Bradford Book – MIT Press, London-Cambridge Mass. 2008, pp. 85-137.

185 M. Tomasello, *The Cultural Origins of Human Cognition.* Harvard University Press, 1999

186 C.J. Lumsden, E.O. Wilson, *Genes, Mind and Culture: The Coevolutionary Process*, Harvard University Press, Cambridge Mass. 1981.

187 R. Dawkins, *Selfish Gene*, Oxford University Press, Oxford 1976; D. Dennett, *Breaking the Spell: Religion as a Natural Phenomenon,* Penguin Group, 2006., pp. 389-405; S. Blackmore, *The Meme Machine*, Oxford University Press, Oxford 2000.

culture, there also appears an aspect of extragenetic transmission of information and behaviour patterns among individuals.

Culture is understood by neoevolutionists in a reductionist way and has its sources in individual behaviour and motivations that, when aggregated, form dominant values and norms in a community[188]. The most important mechanisms of cultural transmission are the learning processes, including imitation, communication, cooperation and other kinds of interaction. Probably, in the case of humanity's ancestors, evolutionary pressure led to positive feedback between the development of social skills and the development of the brain, which translated into fast development of culture[189]. Then, probably already as part of the development of *Homo sapiens*, culture gained more and more importance, allowing for accumulation and transmission of knowledge that helped not only individuals but whole social groups to survive. Innovation related to both material culture (tools, clothes, weapons) and symbolic culture (language, beliefs, social institutions) began to play a key role in the development and growth in size of communities. Biological evolution was to a great extent substituted with a much faster processes of cultural evolution.

The natural origin of culture leads to a description that draws from the context of its creation. Language is deeply rooted in the human spatial and physical understanding of the environment, and some authors even believe it is innate[190]. Most metaphors, similes and designates of abstract notions refer to physical notions[191]. For example, "a superior is above a subordinate", "the market grows", we keep strangers "at a distance" or we treat them "coolly", while our family are the "closest" to us. We show greater ability to understand social processes related to people, as well as to tell stories and narrate, in comparison to abstractions such as the mathematical[192]. We tend to idealise our

188 D.S. Wilson, "Group-Level Evolutionary Processes" in: R.I.M. Dunbar, L. Barrett, *Evolutionary Psychology*, Oxford University Press, New York 2007.

189 C.J. Lumsden, E.O. Wilson, *Promethean Fire: Reflections on the Origin of Mind.* Harvard University Press, Cambridge Mass. 1983; H. Kudo, R.I.M. Dunbar, "Neocortex Size and Social Network Size in Primates", *Animal Behaviour* October 2001, vol. 62, no. 4, pp. 711-722; R.W. Byrne, A. Whiten, *Machiavellian Intelligence: Social Expertise and the Evolution of Intellect in Monkeys, Apes and Humans*, Oxford University Press, New York 1988.

190 S. Pinker, *Language Instinct*, Penguin Books, London 1995.

191 G. Lakoff, M. Johnson, *Metaphors We Live By*, University of Chicago Press, Chicago 1980.

192 P.M. Todd, G. Gigerenzer, "Mechanisms of Ecological Rationality: Heuristics and Environments that Make us Smart" in: R.I.M. Dunbar, L. Barrett, *Evolutionary Psychology*, Oxford University Press, New York 2007.

own group, to be xenophobic, sexist and to stigmatise misfits. According to D. C. Dennett and R. Dawkins, religious beliefs also have evolutionary origins[193].

Within the evolutionary framework, culture can be understood in three ways as: adaptation, an indirect product of evolution, or as its by-product[194]. Adaptations are of a hereditary character and have developed through natural selection, as they are a more efficient solution to the problem of survival or reproduction of individuals than the available alternatives. Animal protocultures evolved in this sense, providing species with hereditary mental modules, allowing them to imitate other individuals. Indirect products do not solve any adaptational or functional problems, as they just accompany other adaptations. It seems that some of the aspects of cultures – like art or beliefs – evolved as indirect products, accompanying the development of cultural adaptations in the form of language or technology. By-products are random variables that – in the evolutionary sense – are of no adaptive importance (such as eye colour, navel shape). Perhaps, in the case of our ancestors, this sphere includes the entire cultural variability, which covers: language structure, type of beliefs, key values and norms. As the importance of cultural evolution in human development grew, the by-products in the evolutionary sense, i.e. the cultural variables of different communities, began to play the key role in the selection of individuals and whole groups[195]. Perhaps, for example more aggressive, better organised or more technologically advanced communities started to gain cultural advantage, becoming the heart of the integration of whole societies.

Culture from the primatological perspective

Language and culture are elements that are uniquely characteristic of mankind, although one can find natural sources for both these phenomena. The great apes use a communication system in order to express their emotions and intentions, and to indicate external threats. However, communication and culture do not have symbolic and abstract aspects characteristic of the language and culture of *Homo sapiens*. Chimpanzees also show aspects of thinking and social, cooperative behaviour, as well as using symbols[196].

---

193 D. Dennett, *Breaking the Spell: Religion as a Natural Phenomenon,* Penguin Group, 2006.; R. Dawkins, , The God Delusion, Bantam Press, London, 2006.

194 D.M. Buss, *Evolutionary Psychology. The New Science of the Mind*, Pearson, Boston 2008, pp. 39-40.

195 R. McElreath, J. Henrich, “Modelling Cultural Evolution” in: R.I.M. Dunbar, L. Barrett, *Evolutionary Psychology*, Oxford University Press, New York 2007.

196 J. Call, “Social Knowledge in Primates” in: R.I.M. Dunbar, L. Barrett, *Evolutionary Psychology*, Oxford University Press, New York 2007.

The position of evolutionists concerning the origins of culture in animal communities is coherent and based on naturalism, i.e. an assumption that human culture is based on biological foundations that can be observed in the protoculture of apes. However, the assessment of the degree of cultural advancement of apes is very diversified. Primatologists, such as F. de Waal or J. Goodall, can see the most important elements of culture in chimpanzees[197]. On the other hand, many psychologists and anthropologists believe that although we can talk of the beginnings of culture in the case of apes, most of its aspects have developed only in the case of mankind[198].

As numerous observations show, apes have a kind of basic moral instinct that has its roots in the essence of a social group, and is of a functional character. Similarly to people, chimpanzees are able to show empathy and liking, altruism, mutuality, feelings of guilt and shame, as well as a sense of fair and equal sharing[199].

Memetic understanding of culture

Memetics has its origin in the general theory of replicators proposed by R. Dawkins, which interprets culture as a process of an algorithmic character, analogous in its course to the evolution of a biological system. The basis of the replicator concept is the assumption that there are structures able to initiate – in appropriate conditions – a process of self-replication of its organisational plan, and under conditions of limited access to resources – by an emergent selection process and, in consequence, evolution. In a given centre, the surviving

197 J. Goodall, *Through a Window: My Thirty Years with the Chimpanzees of Gombe*, Houghton Mifflin, Boston 1990; F. de Waal, A. van Roosmalen, "Reconciliation and Consolation among Chimpanzees", *Behavioral Ecology and Sociobiology* 1979, no. 5, pp. 55-66.

198 J. Vauclair, "Les Animaux pendent-ils?" in: J.F. Dortier, *Le cerveau et la pensée*, Humaines Editions, Paris 2003, p. 215; M. Tomasello, *The Cultural Origins of Human Cognition*. Harvard University Press, 1999

199 F. de Waal, *Good Natured. The Origins of Right and Wrong in Humans and Other Animals*, Harvard University Press, Cambridge Mass. 1996, pp. 133-154; J. Goodall, *Through a Window ...*, op. cit.; F. de Waal, *Primates and Philosophers. How Morality Evolved*, Princeton University Press, Princeton 2006, pp. 161-182; C.M. Korsgaard, "Morality and the Distinctiveness of Human Action" in: F. de Waal, S. Macedo, J. Ober (eds.), *Primates and Philosophers: How Morality Evolved*, Princeton University Press, Princeton 2006, pp. 98-119.

replicators should be the ones that enable the most efficient process of self-replication in comparison with their other versions[200].

Dawkins calls cultural replicators 'memes', from a combination of mimicry (*mimeme*) and genes (*genes*)[201]. Memetics is based on observations carried out by P.F. Jenkins[202] of the mechanisms of variability in the mating songs of birds. He introduced the notion of the "song pool" as a counterpart of the gene pool, as well as "cultural mutations". Thus, the elaboration of the theory of replicators in biology was supposed to be biological evolution together with the perspective of the "selfish gene", while in social sciences, memes were supposed to be the transmitters of culture or, in fact, of all information[203].

However, there are two main approaches to cultural information and the possibility of its transmission within a society[204].

- The gene analogy, which assumes that the accumulation of variability in the process of evolution requires the stability of transmitters of the information coding, and that mimicry is the dominant mechanism of cultural replication[205],
- The viral analogy, which puts an emphasis on the mechanisms of horizontal information flow within a society, as opposed to genes dependant only on the vertical flow; in order to foresee the directions of the evolution of culture's manifestations, it is necessary to apply the basic epidemiological rules[206].

At its current stage of development, memetics is a concept of a mainly qualitative and descriptive character, proven by numerous publications but very little actual research[207]. The empirical material is dominated by research into the phenomenon of the dissemination of chain letters and religious movements. Most research projects related to memetics have been carried out by D. Hofstadter[208] who studied the character of the dissemination of chain letters and

---

200 R. Dawkins, *The Selfish Gene*, Oxford University Press, Oxford 1976, pp. 15-20.

201 Ibid, p. 192.

202 P.F. Jenkins, "Cultural Transmission of Song Patterns and Dialect Development in a Free-Living Bird Population", *Animal Behaviour* 1978, no. 25, pp. 50-78.

203 R. Dawkins, *A Devil's Chaplain*, Weidenfeld & Nicholson, London 2003, p. 251; M. Blute, "Memetics and Evolutionary Social Science", *Journal of Memetics* 2005, no. 19, p. 6.

204 Ibid.

205 R. Dawkins, *The Selfish Gene...*, op. cit., pp. 192-193.

206 R. Dawkins, *Viruses of the Mind*, Blackwell, Cambridge 1993, pp. 48-50.

207 M. Blute, *Memetics and Evolutionary Social Science*, op. cit.

208 D. Hofstadter, *The Mind's I*, Penguin Books, London 1982.

the factors influencing their popularity, and A. Lynch[209] who carried out major research into the mechanisms used by different religious systems and cults in order to increase the number of their followers.

Memetics can be criticised due to its lack of verification. R. Dawkins put forward an ironic accusation towards creationism, ridiculing H. Bergson's idea of *elan vital*[210], saying that researchers could as well state that trains are moved by *elan locomotif*. However, memetics itself is based on a metaphysical assumption that there is a meme which is similar to a gene, i.e. one that gets reproduced and mutated. So far, no one has been able to prove the existence of a 'meme', to measure its effect or to put forward a theory. In this sense, it is an ideology just like the *elan locomotif*, further enhanced emotionally by the stereotype of religion as a "virus of the mind"[211].

Criticism of the neoevolutionary paradigm of culture

A critical view of the concepts of culture related to the neoevolutionary paradigm should take into account two trends. The first refers to empirical research into the process of learning and disseminating information, carried out as a part of evolutionary psychology and supported by primatological observations. The other trend of criticism focuses on the so-called general theory of replication, and especially on its variant concerning culture, i.e. memetics. The trend of criticism of empirical research is moderate, as the results of numerous experiments and observations speak for themselves. However, the criticism of memetics as a new concept of culture is to a large extent legitimate, as in order to become a theory, it should include models of culture and research allowing for its verification.

Many cultural phenomena appearing in psychological research are interpreted in an evolutionary context, but are is not always supported by reliable studies. Brain modules developed by mankind in the Pleistocene were supposed to equip people with the cognitive mechanisms of cultural reproduction, such as symbolic and abstract thinking, emotions, the ability to

---

209 A. Lynch, *Thought Contagion: How Belief Spreads Through Society*, Basic Books, London 1996.

210 R. Dawkins, *Ancestors Tale: A Pilgrimage to the Dawn of Life*, Houghton Mifflin, New York 2004; H. Bergson, L'*énergie spirituelle*. Essais et conférences 1919

211 R. Dawkins, *The God Delusion*, op. cit., cf. P. Boyer, *El l'homme créa les dieux*, Edition Robert Laffont, Paris 2001; D. Dennett, *Breaking the Spell: Religion as a Natural Phenomenon,* Penguin Group, 2006.

show empathy and read minds or the ability to communicate[212]. However, J. Fodor, the originator of the modular mind concept, does not agree with the interpretation indicating a very high level of specialisation of cognitive mechanisms (the so-called penknife concept). Rather, modular minds were supposed to possess general cognitive abilities, and not the algorithms and heuristics of mankind's survival in the Pleistocene[213].

J. Gould ironically describes some of the evolutionary analyses explaining our behaviour as 'just-so stories' – an interpretation *post factum*, which is not a coherent model generating predictions that can be verified. However, this reservation is not fully legitimate, as numerous concepts of learning, imitation and culture developed in the field of evolutionary psychology, give rise to implications in the form of examined human behaviour, which allows for verification of the hypotheses. The same cannot be said about the whole theory of brain modules but, for example, illusions and cognitive limitations that can be deduced from the species' evolution, which are confirmed by research in behavioural economics and evolutionary psychology.

Memetics has been strongly criticised by a number of representatives of the social and biological sciences. Many serious reservations have been voiced, which at the current stage of development make memetics look like an interesting hypothesis, and not a scientific theory. One needs verification which is not easy, taking into consideration the high level of generality of statements and the lack of a model and predictions. The "general theory of replication" is thus only hypothetical and at the moment does not have the form of a mathematical model. So far, no one has been able to identify the transmitter of memes or even indicate the directions of their empirical research[214]. Moreover, memetics still has no uniform and precise definition. Even memes are interpreted differently by different authors[215].

Summary

It seems to me that the marriage of evolutionary thinking and the theory of culture is beginning to bear fruit. On the level of the philosophy of science, it leads to a resignation from the traditional division into social and natural

212 L. Barrett, R. Dunbar, J. Lycett, *Human Evolutionary Psychology*, Palgrave Macmillan, New York 2002, pp. 295-320; D. Sperber, *Explaining Culture*, Blackwell, Oxford 1996.

213 J. Fodor, *The Modularity of Mind: An Essay on Faculty Psychology*, MIT Press, Cambridge Mass. 1983.

214 R. Aunger, *Darwinizing Culture: The Status of Memetics as Science*, Oxford University Press, Oxford 2001, p. 218.

215 K. Distin, *The Selfish Meme*, Cambridge University Press, New York 2005, p. 72.

sciences. The possibility of applying theory and methods of biological sciences related to neuroscience, cognitive science and other fields of natural sciences to cultural issues allows for the study, description, modelling and prediction of cultural changes in a more efficient way. At the same time, I think the position of culture researchers stemming from science should not be orthodox. Many methods and concepts of social sciences developed on the basis of anthropology, sociology, psychology or even philosophy can be useful for cognitive purposes. For example, traditional ethnological methods such as observations and interviews, as well as surveys and statistical methods, still play a very important role in the study of culture. Thus, culture is a kind of epistemological testing ground for combining social and natural sciences, perhaps leading to the end of the traditional division into two cultures[216].

It is also possible that – as the memeticians postulate – research into culture from the perspective of evolutionism will lead to the development of a broad theory of replication, describing the rules of variability in self-replicating systems, regardless of the kind of transmitter (medium). Such a theory would generalise the evolutionary theory, going beyond biological systems and perhaps, from the point of view of scientific development, it would be like the theory of relativity that generalised Newton's theory. However, it is necessary to develop both theoretical and empirical knowledge, and to cross Popper's threshold of epistemological falsifiability. Should this happen, deeper exploration of cultural processes should entail more efficient control of spontaneous, negative ideological phenomena. Thus, the tendency to replicate ideas dangerous to humanity might decrease.

216 C.P. Snow, *The Two Cultures*. London: Cambridge University Press, 1959

Chapter 7
Organisational culture in the neoevolutionary paradigm

Introduction

G. Hofstede assumed that national cultures are a part of people's mental software, which includes the basic values, while organisational cultures are mostly superficial traineeships completed in adulthood[217]. However, it seems organisational cultures are, contrary to Hofstede's belief, very deeply rooted in the human mind and social structures, as they reflect primitive cultures of hunter-gatherer communities, which are inscribed in the mental and genetic 'software' of *Homo sapiens*.

Organisational culture is a problematic research area in the management sciences. Its definitions are ambiguous, there is no agreement as to the paradigm, and the boundary between culture and other areas of management – as well as the assessment of the research methodology's value and the change of organisational culture – are all unclear[218]. Despite doubts of an epistemological and methodological nature, organisational culture is today a deep-rooted notion, commonly used in management. Thus, it seems reasonable to return to the question of the paradigm and the possibility of managing organisational culture.

The studies of the neoevolutionary current, located mainly within evolutionary psychology, shed new light on the interpretation of human behaviour, including organisational behaviour and organisational culture. The aim of this chapter is to present the neoevolutionary interpretations of organisational culture, and to attempt to solve some of the cognitive dilemmas which make it difficult to get to know and manage organisational culture. The thesis of the chapter is that one can draw an analogy between organisational culture and the culture of primitive hunter-gatherer communities.

Darwinian inspirations

Neoevolutionism redefines the essence and origin of culture, rejecting the innately false opposition, deeply rooted in tradition, of culture vs. nature. In fact,

217 Hofstede, G., Hofstede, G.J., *Cultures and Organizations. Software of the Mind,* (2nd edn). New York: McGraw-Hill, 2005, p. 299.

218 Ł. Sułkowski, "Czy warto zajmować się kulturą organizacyjną?", *Zarządzanie zasobami ludzkimi* 2008, no. 6.

cultures developed based on the biology of mankind and all manifestations of human social life are derived from nature and have their origins in the behaviour of primates[219]. Communication and language were formed as a result of animal signals developing into a sophisticated system of transmitting emotions and abstract notions, that then started to evolve itself[220]. Hierarchy, power and leadership, which have contributed to the creation of the complex social structures of today's mass societies, are rooted in the fight for domination and the pecking order of social species[221]. Concern for family and relatives stems from the universal, natural instinct to reproduce one's own genetic material[222]. Collaboration and formation of coalitions between non-kin take place in many species of apes and are the manifestations of a survival strategy based on cooperation[223].

Customs, traditions and rituals being part of each culture seem to be natural norms that regulate the functioning of social species. The studies of neoevolutionism, neoevolutionary psychology, socio-biology, neuroscience, primatology and cognitive science are explaining more and more of the phenomena present in human social life, deriving them directly from the evolutionary mechanisms of *Homo sapiens*[224]. Therefore, it would be worth carrying out a similar analysis in relation to organisational culture.

The evolutionary basis of organisational culture

The biological and evolutionary basis of culture underlies the social nature of mankind. It is a kind of feedback between rivalry and cooperation. Rivalry is related to the ultimate values of the existence of biological species, which – according to neoevolutionists – are genetic reproduction and the survival of individuals. On the other hand, cooperation is an effective mechanism that enhances the chances of survival for genes and individuals.

An analysis of evolutionary sources of human culture reveals that there is an cumulative effect of symbolic works in primitive communities, handed down from generation to generation. Over hundreds of thousands of years, hunter-

---

219 D. Sperber, *Explaining Culture*, Blackwell, Oxford 1996.

220 T.W. Deacon, *The Symbolic Species. The Co-Evolution of Language and the Brain*, W.W. Norton, New York 1997.

221 R. Boyd, P.J. Richerson, "Punishment Allows the Evolution of Cooperation in Sizable Groups", *Ethnology and Sociobiology* 1992, no. 13, pp. 171-195.

222 A. Hughes, *Evolution and Human Kinship*, Oxford University Press, Oxford 1988.

223 S. Bowles, H. Gintis, "Homo Reciprocans", *Nature* 2002, no. 415, pp. 125-128.

224 *Missing the Revolution. Darwinism for Social Scientists*, J. Barkow (ed.), Oxford University Press, Oxford 2006.

gatherer groups initiated a certain organisational culture, characterised by common values, languages and communication systems, beliefs, social norms, customs, traditions and rituals, social role models and taboos, all of which were transferred between generations. Such a cultural system had its origin in the evolutionary biology of mankind, and provided additional, positive feedback which helped form and adopt solutions that were more functional from the perspective of survival of individuals and communities. The cultural bond in small human communities was based on: kinship, non-kinship cooperation, and group identity, based upon the fact the one's own group was distinct from others[225].

One can draw an analogy between primitive hunter-gatherer culture and modern organisational culture. Thus, it seems that informal organisational culture is a natural and very old way of people adjusting to life in a social group. On the one hand, it explains the spontaneous mechanism forming organisational cultures in modern companies and other organisations, and on the other, the difficulty controlling the directions of the culture development. *Homo sapiens* identify themselves with relatively small groups, dominated by informal communication and direct contact. Identifying oneself with larger social groups, such as societies, nations or a religious community, takes the form of a projection of processes transferred from the small group to a mass group. This is the source of stereotypes and the lack of functionality in the actions of large social groups[226]. Organisational culture is thus inscribed in human nature, which management should take it into consideration in the activity of all kinds of organisations.

Functions of organisational culture

Analyses and studies of 'soft' areas of management use the notion of organisational culture functions. The integration function consists in uniting an organisation's members into a community (metaphorically speaking, it is the 'organisational glue'), while the perceptual function is the perception of the organisation itself and its environment in accordance with the values and norms of the culture it is part of (metaphorically speaking, these are 'organisational glasses'). The adaptive function is the socialisation of the community members

225 M. van Vugt, G. Roberts, Ch. Hardy, "Competitive Altruism: A Theory of Reputation-Based Cooperation in Groups" in: R.I.M. Dunbar, L. Barrett, *Evolutionary Psychology*, Oxford University Press, New York 2007.

226 F. Salter, "Ethnic Nepotism as Heuristic: Risky Transactions and Public Altruism" in: R.I.M. Dunbar, L. Barrett, *Evolutionary Psychology*, op.cit.

in accordance with the rules of its functioning, while the function of granting identity is related to the self-identification of the community members[227].

Primitive communities based their unity on: kinship bonds, non-kinship cooperation, leadership, communication and hostility towards other groups. Kinship was one of the strongest sources of social order, although the mechanism of sexual selection also required the development of cooperation with non-kin. The strength of kinship bonds is reflected in the nepotism and familism present in a number of modern organisational cultures. In primitive groups the hierarchy of power was established on authority, seniority and often social coalitions too, which is translated into reproduction, access to goods and the possibility of sanctioning.

This is reflected in culture in formal and informal organisational hierarchies with their symbolic and material attributes of power and leadership. The culture of primitive groups – similar to modern organisational culture – socialises the community members, giving them identity and forming intentional perception. Thus, there is a clear similarity between the functions of primitive group culture and the features of organisational culture in modern companies and institutions.

Dimensions of organisational culture's values

The values being the basis for the creation of culture are defined in different ways. In the case of organisational culture, some authors assume that it has certain values that are not found in other cultures, such as the national or regional[228]. Other researchers believe that the dimensions of cultural values are rather of a universal character, and that they can be described on the level of the culture of societies and organisations. Assuming the latter perspective, one can point to a number of different descriptions of the values' dimensions. The dimensions of cultural values used in the most important research by G. Hofstede, A. Trompenaars, Ch. Hampden-Turner and R. J. House are: individualism – collectivism, power distance, avoiding uncertainty and masculinism – feminism[229]. From the neoevolutionary perspective one can see that these values are rooted in the "human nature".

227 C. Sikorski, *Kultura organizacyjna w instytucji*, Wydawnictwo Uniwersytetu Łódzkiego, Łódź 1990, pp. 13-16.

228 G. Hofstede, G.J. Hofstede, *Cultures and Organizations.* op. cit., pp. 299-307.

229 G. Hofstede, *Culture's Consequences*, Sage Publications, Beverly Hills 1984; Ch. Hampden-Turner, A. Trompenaars, Riding the waves of culture: understanding cultural diversity in business. London: Nicholas Brealey, 1997; R.J. House, P. Hanges, A. Ruiz-Quintanilla, *GLOBE. The Global Leadership and Organizational Behavior. Effectiveness: Research Program* 1997.

The formation of human identity stems from the evolutionary development of a functional community, based on the ability to recognise differences between oneself and others, as well as between fellows and strangers. This is why the attitude of an individual towards the community as a whole becomes an existential problem. The behaviour of *Homo sapiens* includes a whole range of egoistic and altruistic actions which result from two different strategies of achieving evolutionary success, measured by the reproduction and survival of individuals. Individualistic culture leads to the enhancement of selfish motivations, while collectivist cultures enhance altruism towards the members of one's own community. Thus, individualisation is based on evolution and is related to the appearance of ego and a characteristic composition of individual behavioural features[230]. In the process of the individualisation of individuals and communities, the key role is played by attributes characteristic only of mankind, such as the sense of time (temporal dimension of the ego) and abstract thinking[231].

Power is inscribed in human nature and reveals itself in different ways: pecking order, formation of hierarchy, leadership in groups, the willingness to gain control over others, creation of material and symbolic attributes of power, as well as cooperation based on social order.

Power distance indicates an imaginary, symbolic space that separates those in power from their subordinates. It translates into the level of autocracy and cooperation, and the type of sanctions (e.g. physical, symbolic). Power in a human society is perceived in dualistic terms as an attribute and a relation.

The tolerance of uncertainty is related to a mental feature developed to the greatest extent in humans, i.e. awareness of the past. Animals, including probably the great apes, can extrapolate from the past only to a limited degree. People are deeply aware of the unpredictability of the future, including their own inevitable ends. The unpredictability of the future and the risks it entails are sources of uncertainty which lead to stress. Being an emotional response to dangerous situations, stress is evolutionarily inherited from the distant ancestors of mankind. However, the abstract source of stress in the form of a fear of the future is characteristic only of people. Avoiding uncertainty is a universal

---

230 D. Nettle, "Individual differences" in: R.I.M. Dunbar, L. Barrett, *Evolutionary Psychology*, op.cit.

231 M. Schaller, J.H. Park, D.T. Kenrick, "Human Evolution and Social Cognition" in: R.I.M. Dunbar, L. Barrett, *Evolutionary Psychology*, op. cit.; J.J. Skowronski, C. Sedikides, "Temporal Knowledge and Autobiographical Memory: An Evolutionary Perspective" in: R.I.M. Dunbar, L. Barrett, *Evolutionary Psychology*, op. cit.

feature of *Homo sapiens*, while the level of the fear and stress experienced depends on the culture and individuals[232].

Attitudes towards the opposite sex, reflected in the opposition between masculinism and feminism, are connected with sexual relations and gender identity. G. Hofstede assumed a completely different understanding of this dimension and focused on the aim and quality of life[233]. Still, many other authors return to the fundamental problem of relations between sexes, both from the biological perspective (sex) and the cultural (gender). The neoevolutionary analysis points to the most important aspects of relations between the sexes, i.e. the diversification of reproduction and life strategies, sex, the relations of submission and threats of violence[234]. Sex differences determine the strategies for winning partners and parental strategies; they also condition the directions of personality development and life trajectories of individuals[235].

Thus, if the value dimensions develop on the universal grounds of human nature, where does their diversity relative to culture and individuals come from? For example, some cultures have large power distance (Mexico), while others small (USA), or in the case of some, the level of individualism is high (USA), and in others the same can be said about collectivism (China)[236]. It seems that diverse histories of societies understood as communities identifying with themselves have led to a strengthening of certain values and weakening of others. This, then, is why cultures have diversified on the universal basis of human nature and its existential problems; power, attitude towards the group, attitude towards the past and relations between sexes, as some of these have developed under conditions of group work, like the culture of rice pickers, or formed as collectivism or a cult of pioneers and individuals[237].

---

232 B. Winterhalder, "Risk and Decision-Making" in: R.I.M. Dunbar, L. Barrett, *Evolutionary Psychology*, op. cit.

233 G. Hofstede, G.J. Hofstede, *Cultures and Organizations*, op. cit., p. 133.

234 D. Kimura, *Sex and cognition,* The MIT Press, *1999*; A. Campbell, "Sex Differences in Aggression" in: R.I.M. Dunbar, L. Barrett, *Evolutionary Psychology*, op. cit.

235 B.S. Low, "Ecological and Socio-Cultural Impacts on Mating Marriage Systems" in: R.I.M. Dunbar, L. Barrett, *Evolutionary Psychology*, op. cit.; J. Belsky, "Childhood Experiences and Reproductive Strategies" in: R.I.M. Dunbar, L. Barrett, *Evolutionary Psychology*, op. cit.; S. W. Gangestad, "Reproductive Strategies and Tactics" in: R.I.M. Dunbar, L. Barrett, *Evolutionary Psychology*, op. cit.

236 G. Hofstede, G.J. Hofstede, *Cultures and Organizations*, op. cit., pp. 57 and 91.

237 G. Morgan, Images of Organization, Newbury Park, CA: Sage, 1986, pp. 129-130.

Elements of organisational cultures

Anthropological research provides rich empirical materials that allow description of elements of organisational cultures by analogy with primitive hunter-gatherer groups. Organisational ethnology developed from the methodology of field research, drawing directly from the research of cultural anthropology. The elements common to both organisational cultures and primitive groups on an advanced level of development are: social values and norms, speech and a communication system, stories and myths, beliefs, customs, traditions and rituals, role models (heroes, family roles), and taboos[238]. If one adopts broad, enumerative definitions of culture, they would also include art, art material products (e.g. architecture), morality, power structure and the system of ideas.

The previously described cultural values, related to solving basic existential dilemmas (attitude towards the community, power, fear of the future and relations between sexes), result in a system of norms, i.e. dictates and prohibitions that regulate community life. Norms become rooted and consolidated, gaining functional forms with time, which favour the survival of individuals and the community, though their petrifaction in the face of changes in external conditions may lead to a weakening of their functionality. In the case of organisational culture, norms stem from implemented and undeclared values, so they are functional, but in relation to the actual system of values and not always assumed by those in charge. Social norms should not question the basic value that implicitly underlies each form of organisation, which is related to the individual pursuit of survival and genetic reproduction.

Communication systems, language and speech are developed from more primitive forms of communication and signalling used by different animals. However, language is characterised by the possibility to code and transfer theoretically unlimited amounts of complex, abstract, information. The development of speech, language and communication has provided people with a sophisticated tool supporting the survival and development of mankind. The development of speech is closely related to the development of the brain, and is probably reflected in the human genome[239]. In the beginning, communication enabled the transfer of ideas and the accumulation of achievements, the development of symbolic culture, more efficient hunting, a higher level of security, and the improvement of tools. In short, it became the cornerstone of

---

238 L.G. Bolman, T.E. Deal, *Reframing Organizations, Artistry, Choice and Leadership*, Jossey-Bass, San Francisco 2003, pp. 241-269.

239 Ch. Kenneally, *The First Word. The Search for the Origins of Language*, Viking Penguin, New York 2007, pp. 267-270.

mankind. The cultures of communities create their own languages, which serve integration and communication purposes. The rhetorical figures, metaphors, and language humour that people use form a cognitive framework which includes different cultural circles. The notion of the 'spirit' of a language conveys the specificity of a communication system, in which form shapes message. The development of language contributed to the creation and dissemination of beliefs, stories, myths and taboos, which form a thick tapestry of symbolic culture. The cave-dwelling ancestors of people were immersed in it, just like today's people are in organisational culture.

Culture also produces social role models, starting from those in charge, through subordinates, and ending with family and parental roles. Within organisational cultures one can distinguish the roles of heroes, offering models of behaviour from the point of view of leadership, with which the organisation's members identify themselves.

Typologies of organisational cultures

Primitive hunter-gatherer communities are described from the angle of the works of material culture, which on a certain level also reflects the complexity of symbolic thinking. Tools, burial methods, cave paintings and other archaeological remains allow characterisation of the level of complexity of a given local culture, but usually speak little of the actual structure of those groups. Thus, the interpretations of Cro-Magnon cultures, for example, are rather limited[240].

Reference books offer a number of typologies of organisational cultures. The most popular are the classifications by T.E. Deal and A.A. Kennedy, and by Ch. Handy.

T.E. Deal and A.A. Kennedy presented the typology of organisational culture based on two dimensions: feedback speed and the degree of decision risk. The combination of these two parameters gave rise to four types of organisational culture: tough-guy (rapid feedback and high risks), work-hard, play-hard (rapid feedback and low risk), bet-the-company culture (slow feedback and high risk) and process culture (slow feedback and low risk)[241]. These four types of culture are also called: the culture of individualism, culture

240 Ch. Stringer, R. McKie, *African Exodus*. Henry Holt and company, New York, 1997, pp. 245-250.

241 T.E. Deal, A.A. Kennedy, *Corporate Cultures: The Rites and Rituals of Corporate Life*, Penguin Books, Harmondsworth 1982.

of routine, culture of gambling and balanced culture[242]. Analysing this typology from the point of view of neoevolutionism, one can compare the cultures to the functioning of a primitive group. The tough-guy culture may have its origin in a risky team game of hunters; the work-hard culture is equivalent to the gathering activities of primitive communities; the bet-the-company culture is related to the focus on rivalry for prestige and power within the group, while the process culture means subordination.

The second most popular typology of organisational cultures was presented by Ch. Handy[243]. It distinguishes four types of culture orientations: power culture is characterised by the lack of formal rules and procedures of action. It's management is of an autocratic character with power strongly centralised, and employees are driven by rivalry. Role culture is distinguished by rationalism and order. Great significance is attached to the predictability of behaviour and formal rules and employees are expected to be stable and serious – employee activity and initiative are undesirable. The source of power in this organisation is in the organisational hierarchy. Task culture values achievement of objectives. Private needs are suppressed and everyone focuses on the team and team work. Power is based on the competence of the leader. The basis for person culture is the belief that organisations are created in order to serve the needs of individuals. It gives individuals large freedom in their actions, and this type of culture has no mechanisms of control and hierarchy, apart from a bilateral agreement.

Using the neoevolutionary perspective allows us to link the classification by Ch. Handy to the culture of primitive hunter-gatherer groups. Power culture has its origin in striving for dominance, which translated into evolutionary success in the form of reproduction and survival; role culture mostly means subordination to the hierarchy and social roles; task culture concentrates on harmonious cooperation, efficiency and community cohesion, while person culture is a relatively casual coalition of cooperating individuals.

Summary

The culture of hunter-gatherer communities was created in primitive groups and gave rise to the mechanisms for accumulating works and transmitting values,

242 G. Jones, "Enhancing Due Diligence – Examination of the Organisational Culture of a Merger and Acquisition Target", *Journal of Business & Economics Research* 2008, vol. 6, no. 1, p. 13.

243 C.B. Handy, *Understanding Organisations*, 3rd ed., Penguin Books, Harmondsworth 1985.

norms and cultural models. In this sense, all other types of culture reflect the features of the primitive culture, rooted in human nature in the process of evolution[244]. It seems that organisational culture is a natural field of culture, developing spontaneously in organisations and reflecting the evolutionary past of mankind (Table 7).

Between organisational culture and the culture of primitive communities there are numerous analogies. However, there are also significant differences.

1. Organisational culture is just one of many cultural fields, and is entangled in the correlations between them. The relations between national or regional culture and organisational culture are subject to a number of studies. The culture of primitive groups is a homogeneous culture, providing its members with one type of identity. Thus, modern people function within numerous cultural identities, while our distant ancestors identified themselves with one type of group (albeit one which may have included several subcultures, related to, for example, kinship).
2. Organisational culture is a product of intentional, secondary social groups, while the culture of hunter-gatherer communities was created in primary groups that emerged spontaneously. Primitive groups are of an organic character; they are formed spontaneously and are subject to informal, traditional and thoroughly cultural regulations. They are dominated by direct contact, oral communication and the full involvement of their members in the life of the group. Secondary groups are of a deliberate and arbitrary character, and have formalised, business-like bonds.
3. Organisational culture can be formed by those in charge through conscious use of the tools of change, although the scope of intervention is limited. The culture of primitive communities developed spontaneously, so the results of its changes were unpredictable, and the influence of a leader was not conscious.

244 Cf. R. Conniff, *The Ape in the Corner Office*, Cyan Communications Ltd., New York 2008.

Table 7. Analogies between the culture of hunter-gatherer communities and organisational culture

Criterion	Culture of hunter-gatherer communities	Organisational culture
1	2	3
Group size	From several dozen to about 150 individuals	Unlimited, but communities crystallise from several dozen to 150 individuals[245]
Type of social bond	Only direct, kin and non-kin	Direct and indirect, kin and non-kin
Type of power	Informal, hierarchical, based on authority (legitimised by cooperation)	Formal and informal, based on authority (legitimised rationally, legally or by cooperation)
Type of cooperation	Cooperation combined with rivalry	Cooperation combined with rivalry
Values	Existential dimensions: attitude towards the community, power, fear of the future and relations between sexes	Existential dimensions, Dimensions characteristic of the organisation (imposed on the employees as part of secondary socialisation)
Functions of the culture	Integration, perception, identification, granting identity	Integration, perception, identification, granting identity
Culture typologies	Related to chronology and complexity of material art works	Taking into consideration diverse dimensions of culture
Language, communication and myths	Characteristic language serving information and emotive purposes	Characteristic language serving information and emotive purposes
Social roles, archetypes, heroes	Leader, subordinates, parental roles, children's roles, sexual roles, neighbour roles	Leader, subordinates, many other roles depending on the organisation
Research methodology in the culture, derived from different disciplines	Archaeology, cultural anthropology, evolutionary psychology	Organisational anthropology

Source: Own study.

245 M. Gladwell, *The Tipping Point. How Little Things Can Make a Big Difference*, Little, Brown and Company, New York 2000, pp. 177-181.

Our knowledge of organisational cultures is a rich one, because it comes from copious modern research using diverse methodologies. Knowledge about the cultures of primitive communities is fragmentary and limited due to scant source materials and temporal distance. Thus, analyses taking into consideration primitive hunter-gatherer communities tend to be of a speculative character. However, I think that in light of the development of research carried out by evolutionary psychology and other disciplines, cultural studies cannot ignore the heritage of mankind.

Chapter 8
Neoevolutionary Concept of Power

Introduction

Power is one of the most important and the oldest problems of social sciences and the humanities. Since antiquity, philosophers have deliberated on the issue of political power and just ruling. The specialisation of sciences in the 19th and 20th centuries has led to a situation where research into power was carried out as part of several fields of the social sciences, including sociology, political science, cultural anthropology, psychology and law. Although nowadays there are many more empirical studies, it would still be difficult to say that a coherent theory of power, used by the different sciences, has been developed. Modern research of primatology and neuroscience sheds new light on the issue of power, so it is justified to include these disciplines in the discourse of science concerning power and hierarchy.

Universal sources of power

Power and hierarchy are the basic indicators of social structures, which emerge spontaneously in human communities. The social structures themselves, including all manifestations of power, are created culturally. However, as numerous studies show, originally they are of an evolutionary character[246]. Power, understood as the striving for control over the behaviour of other individuals and the possibility to impose one's will on them, is deeply rooted in animal communities. Drawing experience from the world of biology, one could ask, in which kinds of animal communities we indeed deal with power? If we assume that an individual has to have a will, we exclude the whole sphere of instinct and impulses from the area of power. In this sense, there is no power in insect communities, as they do not show even the beginnings of consciousness and will. The behaviour of ants or bees is based solely on automatism. However, in the case of animals that do have consciousness, such as primates, we can talk about power.

Hierarchy is present in all communities. It is manifested in the structure and order that regulate the functioning of the society, in which individuals and groups play various roles. In the case of species that have no consciousness, the

246 M.V. Flinn, "Evolution of Stress Response to Social Threat" in: R.I.M. Dunbar, L. Barrett, *Evolutionary Psychology*, Oxford University Press, New York 2007.

roles are determined genetically, although the catalyst which activates the functions of individual genes is usually the environment. In some primates' communities, hierarchy results from the coexistence of a natural structuralisation process and active power plays between individuals and their coalitions. In human societies, hierarchy is to a large extent based on cultural factors combined with power plays. However, the cultural context of exercising power is of a clearly evolutionary origin. In many societies the cultural rules support nepotism, strengthen masculinity and favour individuals who display a high level of dominance. At the same time, the cultural universalism of human communities are the mechanisms compensating for the abuse of power, such as social sanctions (exclusion, punishment), compensation, as well as the moral sense[247].

The question of the genesis of power in animal communities is very controversial. However, there is a probable relation between power and hierarchy, inequality, systems of dominance, and predating them – aggression and territorialism. A system based on dominance can be defined from the behavioural perspective as the number of permanent aggressive/submissive relations between animals[248]. In the case of social species, being at the top of the hierarchy entails natural benefits related to the most important stakes in the 'game of life', survival and reproduction.

Animals that reveal at least the beginnings of consciousness will try to achieve the highest possible position in their hierarchy, at the same time calculating their resources. In the case of many societies, the rule of hierarchisation is very simple: the strongest individuals dominate. Research on numerous mammals (e.g. wolves) shows that their strong hierarchisation is related to developing, following or even learning their norms from a young age. Many researchers believe that hierarchisation and adaptability were the reasons for the quick domestication of dogs[249]. Primatological research shows that in communities of chimpanzees and bonobos, the alpha male is usually an individual forming coalitions with others[250]. Thus, power among many primates is based on manipulating others and cooperation, rather than aggression and violence.

One of the concepts of the development of hominid communities is the hypothesis of Machiavellian intelligence, according to which, in the course of

---

247 D.E. Brown, *Human Universals*, McGraw-Hill, New York 1991.

248 E.O. Wilson, *Sociobiology: The New Synthesis*, Harvard University Press, 2000.

249 F. de Waal, *Good Natured. The Origins of Right and Wrong in Humans and Other Animals*, Harvard University Press, Cambridge Mass.-London 1996, pp. 94-95.

250 J. Goodall, *The Chimpanzees of Gombe: Patterns of Behaviour*, Bellknap Press of the Harvard University Press, Boston 1986.

the evolution of our ancestors, the key selection factor was their skill in social manipulation[251]. Statistically, individuals who are able to perceive others' intentions, form coalitions and alliances, deceive others and make it difficult for them to predict their behaviour, occupied higher positions in hominid groups, which translated into evolutionary success[252].

Apart from primatological research, work on neuronal interpretations of power- holding are also well under way. It seems that this process includes both cerebral regions related to aggression, and mirror neurons considered to be the basis for empathy and cooperation[253]. Regardless of the opinion of the Machiavellian intelligence concept, there is no doubt that power in human communities is formed on a biological basis. At the same time, thanks to the development of societies, organisations, formal social institutions etc., the development of power has taken a course characteristic only of human communities, one not present in the case of other animals.

Power and culture

Despite its evolutionary foundations, power in human communities is also conditioned by culture. Most intercultural, comparative studies take into consideration different approaches to power in different communities. For example, the research by G. Hofstede, Ch. Hampden-Turner and A. Trompenaars, as well as by R. Inglehart, R. House and his team reveals that cultures differ in terms of power distance. Power distance can be understood as the degree of subordination and manifestation of submission by subordinates considered normal in a given culture. Despite the discrepancies in the results, all projects indicate that relatively high power distance is characteristic of societies in, for example, Central and South America (Mexico, Argentina, Chile), while relatively speaking, the smallest power distance is found in Scandinavian countries (Sweden, Denmark)[254]. It is worth emphasising that studies of cultural

251 A. Whiten, R.W. Byrne (eds.), *Machiavellian Intelligence II: Extensions and Evaluations*, Cambridge University Press, Cambridge 1997.

252 *Machiavellian Intelligence II*, op. cit., pp. 144-173.

253 G. Rizzolatti, L. Fogassi, "Mirror neurons and social cognition" in: R.I.M. Dunbar, L. Barrett, *Evolutionary Psychology*, Oxford University Press, New York 2007; V. Gallese, A. Goldman, "Mirror Neurons and the Stimulation Theory of Mind-Reading", *Trends in Cognitive Sciences* 1998, no. 12, pp. 493-501.

254 G. Hofstede, *Culture's Consequences*, Sage Publications, Beverly Hills 1984; Ch. Hampden-Turner, A. Trompenaars, *Riding the waves of culture: understanding cultural diversity in business*, London: Nicholas, 1997; R.J. House, P. Hanges, A. Ruiz-Quintanilla, *GLOBE. The Global Leadership and Organizational Behavior. Effective-*

diversity indirectly confirm the thesis of moderate cultural universalism; and hierarchy can be found in all known and studied communities, although they have different forms and intensity.

The issue of cultural determinants of power leads to philosophical questions about whether culture is the source of social contract, and whether it tones down the excesses of power. In troops of chimpanzees the possibility of abusing power is usually limited. Admittedly, primatologists describe the evolutionary benefits of occasional outbursts of uncontrolled anger for dominant individuals, however, staying in power requires cooperation and coalitions, and therefore a certain degree of acceptance by a large part of the group. Thus, in the case of chimpanzees and bonobos, power is not based on tyranny, although violence is one of the most often used attributes[255]. Only specialisation and distribution of work, technological development and an increase in the size of human communities enables abuse of power on a large scale.

It seems that the roots of many manifestations of social life that are related to power have certain important features that have not changed since the times of our evolutionary ancestors. These are mostly war, aggression and violence, relations between the sexes, the idea of justice and equality, and the relationship between power and ownership.

Aggression and violence

Aggression and violence are induced both culturally and biologically. Aggression is a kind of quick response to threats and an alternative to escape. The aim of aggressive behaviour is scaring off or wounding an opponent, and sometimes even killing them. The initiation of aggression is strongly emotional and is related to psychophysical stress. The consequence of aggressive reaction is also a narrowing of the perception and limiting of rational thinking ("blindness")[256]. In animal communities, aggression always has a physical form (attack, chase), although it is often of a ritualistic character and does not aim at wounding the opponent. People, apart from physical forms, also use certain forms of indirect cultural symbolic aggression (insults, invectives, shaking fists etc.), which do not change the essence of the physiological reaction.

---

ness: Research Program, Polish Psychological Bulletin 1997, no. 28(3), pp. 215-254; R. Inglehart, *Modernization and Postmodernization. Cultural, Economic and Political Change in 43 Societies*, Princeton University Press, New Jersey 1997.

255 F. de Waal, *Good Natured...*, op. cit.

256 M. Gladwell, *Blink: The Power of Thinking of Thinking Without Thinking*, Time Warner Book Group, New York 2005.

Primatological research in chimpanzees shows that the alpha males are usually rather aggressive individuals, although not the most aggressive. It seems that a higher level of aggression helps in competing and fighting for power, but a too-high level diminishes the ability to cooperate, form coalitions and alliances, and leads to "blindness"[257]. The level of violence and aggression in a community of chimpanzees is much higher than in human society, and this is probably an important factor regulating social order; aggressive individuals then have a greater chance of reproducing. On the other hand, bonobos (the second living species of chimpanzees) are gentler and use violence or behave in an aggressive way less often. It's probable here that the key factor regulating social order in the case of bonobos is sexual intercourse. To put it trivially, one could say that the keys to exercising power among primates are sex and violence.

Homo sapiens, at least from the genetic perspective, are as closely related to chimpanzees as to bonobos[258]. The patterns of aggression and violence in people are complex and changeable, but they show certain similarities which are a consequence of evolution:

1. On average, men are more aggressive and prone to use violence than women[259];
2. There are patterns of aggressive behaviour characteristic of different sexes, age groups and status groups, e.g. the aggression of male youth groups, the aggression of young women, the aggression of superiors towards their subordinates[260];
3. There are patterns of aggressive behaviour related to threats, such as the aggression of women defending their children[261];
4. The degree of kinship is inversely proportional to the use of violence[262];
5. Functioning in a homogenous group enhances the tendency to use violence,

---

257 F. de Waal, *Good Natured...*, op. cit.

258 R. Dawkins, *Ancestors Tale: A Pilgrimage to the Dawn of Life*, Houghton Mifflin, New York 2004.

259 M. Wilson, M. Daly, "Competitiveness, Risk Taking, and Violence: The Young Male Syndrome" in: *The Functional Mind. Readings in Evolutionary Psychology*, D.T. Kenrick, C.L. Luce (eds.), Pearson, Boston 2004.

260 A. Campbell, "A Few Good Men: Evolutionary Psychology and Female Adolescent Aggression" in: *The Functional Mind. Readings in Evolutionary Psychology*, D.T. Kenrick, C.L. Luce (eds.), Pearson, Boston 2004.

261 F. de Waal, *Good Natured...*, op. cit.

262 M. Wilson, M. Daly, "Competitiveness, Risk Taking, and Violence...", op. cit.

6. The feeling of being threatened by another group increases the probability of using violence.

Primates wars

For a very long time, wars were believed to be the sole purview of the human domain. Wars present group members with considerable cognitive, communication and organisational challenges. They are also related to intentional, deliberate actions that show the signs of conscious planning. Furthermore, wars are incredibly risky and costly, although they offer undeniable evolutionary benefits (as they increase evolutionary fitness)[263]. However, the research by J. Goodall and many other authors has explicitly proved that chimpanzees also engage in wars[264]. 'War' is here understood as a regular, mutual use of group violence towards the representatives of a different group, the aim of which is to destroy that group as a whole and incorporate its resources. In troops of primates it is a group undertaking which, from the statistical point of view, benefits its participants. The chimpanzees of Gombe fought with neighbouring troops, launching group attacks on the males from other troops, seriously wounding or killing isolated individuals. After a defeated group was disintegrated, the males took over its females. The levels of aggression and violence towards other troops and strange individuals were much higher than they were towards the representatives of their own group. It seems then, that such an attitude may be interpreted as a biological source of xenophobia.

Primatological research and the interpretations of evolutionary psychologists show that there are a number of variables that increase the possibility of an outbreak of war, which are related to its adaptive function:

1. The degree of certainty of victory;
2. The certainty as to the random distribution of the risk of death or getting wounded among the members of one's own group;
3. The certainty of a relatively 'fair' distribution of spoils (food, sexual and territorial resources);
4. The effectiveness of using reproduction resources.

---

263 J. Tooby, L. Cosmides, *The Evolution of War and its Cognitive Foundations*, Institute for Evolutionary Studies Technical Report 1988, no. 88, p. 1.

264 R.W. Wrangham, "The Evolution of Social Structures" in: *Primate Societies*, B.B. Smuts, D.L. Cheney, R.M. Seyfarth, R.W. Wrangham, T.T. Struhsaker (eds.), Chicago University Press, Chicago 1987, pp. 282-296; J. Goodall, *The Chimpanzees of Gombe...*, op.cit.

J. Tooby and L. Cosmides believe that the presence of these factors supports participation in coalitions of fighting males, compensating for the threat to life[265]. Forming cooperative coalitions of males was related to enthusiasm and excitement, which compensated for the uncertainty, risk and feeling of threat. Evolutionary psychologists see this as the source of war enthusiasm, excitement with group actions, war and fight daze[266].

Aggression and war are ways to increase power despite access to limited resources. War as aggression aimed outside the group is an additional source of authority and allows selection of leaders who possess the highest level of Machiavellian intelligence.

Sex and power relations

Research shows that although striving for power and aggression are species features, there is a clear difference between the sexes[267]. The aggregated results of social research confirm the stereotype that men are greedier for power and more aggressive than women. However, this does not mean that women lack the ambition to exercise power or aggressiveness[268]. Quite the opposite, in the last few decades, the level of violence among women in most countries has increased. This is yet more proof that evolutionary factors are inseparably linked to cultural factors in determining social actions.

Observation of chimpanzees has shown that males resort to violence and aggression much more often, trying to achieve a higher position in their hierarchy. On the one hand, it is the fight for dominance in a troop, although in this case cooperation and forming alliances are more important than violence. On the other hand, aggression is intensified by taking part in wars. Females do not participate in wars due to different reproductive strategies. However, representatives of both sexes engage in the competition for resources from an early age[269]. In victory, males – thanks to access to females from conquered troops – gain the possibility to reproduce, while females gain nothing in this respect and would just be risking their lives. Differences in reproductive strategies are also one of the main reasons for 'natural' sources of rape. Since

---

265 J. Tooby, L. Cosmides, *The Evolution of War and its Cognitive Foundation*, op. cit.

266 Ibid., p. 7.

267 A. Campbell, "Sex Differences in Aggression" in: R.I.M. Dunbar, L. Barrett, *Evolutionary Psychology*, Oxford University Press, New York 2007.

268 A. Campbell, "A Few Good Men: Evolutionary Psychology and Female Adolescent Aggression", *Ethnology and Sociobiology* 1995, vol. 16, no. 2, pp. 367-381.

269 F.J. Sulloway, "Birth Order and Sibling Competition" in: R.I.M. Dunbar, L. Barrett, *Evolutionary Psychology*, Oxford University Press, New York 2007.

the dawn of mankind, women have been considered part of war spoils. Is the commonness of rape – as suggested by radical feminist movements – the result of men's attempt to terrorise women and maintain patriarchy? [270] The neoevolutionary interpretation is completely different and refers to reproductive strategy[271]. Additionally, research showing that men are much more prone to using sexual violence seems credible (CSX coercive sexuality)[272], and the question of differences in the level of aggression in the sexual behaviour of men and women has been well studied.

However, the issue of the formation of relations of power with reference to sex has been poorly researched and is the source of a number of scientific, political and social controversies. Human societies are moderately monogamous, which is an unusual phenomenon among primates, so it would be difficult to find credible evidence from the perspective of primatology. Most anthropological sources point to the dominance of patriarchal communities and patrilineality as the prevailing pattern of succession[273]. However, there are also numerous researchers who indicate that in many primitive hunter-gatherer communities, women were the ones who chose their partners, which led to sexual selection. Statistically, the most often promoted individuals were cooperative, protective, sociable and credible, while the too-aggressive ones were rejected. One of the evolutionary hypotheses here explicitly shows that the choices and power of women over the reproduction process were indeed factors directing the social development of hominids[274]. Thus, it seems that at the current stage of research we cannot declare that one or other of the sexes is more naturally predestined to hold power.

---

270 S. Brownmiller, *Against our Will: Men, Women and Rape*, Ballantine Books, New York 1993.

271 D.M. Buss, N. Malamuth, *Sex, Power, Conflict: Evolutionary and Feminist Perspectives*, Oxford University Press, Oxford 1996.

272 R. Thornhill, N.W. Thornhill, "The Evolutionary Psychology of Men's Coercive Sexuality", *Behavioral and Brain Sciences* 1992, vol. 15(2), pp. 363-421; R.F. Baumeister, K.R. Catanese, H.M. Wallace, "Conquest by Force: A Narcissistic Reactance Theory of Rape and Sexual Coercion", *Review of General Psychology* 2002, vol. 6(1), pp. 92-135.

273 R. Mace, "The Evolutionary Ecology of Human Family Size" in: R.I.M. Dunbar, L. Barrett, *Evolutionary Psychology*, Oxford University Press, New York 2007; V. Lummaa, "Life-History Theory, Reproduction and Longevity in Humans" in: R.I.M. Dunbar, L. Barrett, *Evolutionary Psychology*, Oxford University Press, New York 2007; E. Voland, "Evolutionary Psychology Meets History: Insights into Human Nature through Family Reconstitution Studies" in: R.I.M. Dunbar, L. Barrett, *Evolutionary Psychology*, Oxford University Press, New York 2007.

274 G. Miller, *The Mating Mind. How Sexual Choice Shaped the Evolution of Human Nature*, Anchor 2000.

Justice in society

Franz de Waal is a supporter of the thesis that the moral sense, including the sense of justice and equality, is of an evolutionary character and can be found not only in chimpanzee communities, but also in many other species. Striving for justice and equality of treatment is one of the ways of maintaining social order. On the one hand, it consists in showing respect to the authority of power represented by the alpha male, while on the other, chimpanzees are able to organise group protests against excessive use of violence within the group. The role of the alpha male is, among others, to separate and reconcile the feuding parties and ensure justice while distributing goods in accordance with the hierarchy.

Observation of chimpanzees has described numerous cases of a group opposing excessive aggression by the alpha male, which often leads to his losing the dominant position. Chimpanzee communities are based on rules and norms respected by the community, including important rules governing power and justice. They also have a wide variety of social sanctions imposed for violation of these norms. The least severe are a kind of reprimand in the form of shouts, threats or slight corporal punishment, while the most severe entail the loss of one's position in the hierarchy, ostracism, serious bodily injury or even expulsion from the troop[275].

Behavioural rules related to power in ape communities include a number of real and ritual types of behaviour of individuals subordinate to dominant ones, such as: bending, turning to face them, soothing gestures, lowering of the voice, coming when being called, following orders and many others forms of showing respect and submission. The dominant individuals have clear privileges concerning the distribution of resources, which is accepted by the group but does not mean that the rules of sharing and reciprocity do not apply to them too[276]. Chimpanzees too have a wide repertoire of emotions, which on the one hand help them to achieve higher positions in their hierarchies, and on the other, enhance their sense of justice and the need to maintain their social structures. Their emotional range includes happiness, pleasure, anger, anxiety, and also strong, socially-induced emotions, such as shame and guilt. Primatological research clearly shows that chimpanzees and bonobos have innate respect for power, the rule of hierarchy, the rules of justice and social order. The alpha male is only one of numerous elements of this moral and social proto-system.

In the context of the presented deliberations, an idealised image of a chimpanzee community emerges, resembling a community of happy savages, as

---

275 F. de Waal, *Good Natured...*, op. cit., p. 92.

276 Ibid., pp. 150-153.

if taken from the works by J.J. Rousseau. A community that has a natural, Hobbes-like Leviathan, but also an internalised moral sense[277]. It is an incorrect association, as the basis for their development of rules for power and justice was a spontaneous mechanism of balance, providing social individuals with the maximum possibility to reproduce and survive. This is why the repertoire of behaviour related to power also includes behaviour we would classify as anti-social, albeit profitable to the individual. A good example are the sporadic outbursts of aggression in alpha males for no apparent reason, often aimed at randomly chosen, weaker individuals. Their social effects are principally a strengthening of the fear of the dominant figure and punishment in the troop, which activates the mechanisms of self-control in subordinate individuals, but also makes it difficult to predict the behaviour of alpha males and mind-reading, which is the basis for social manipulation.

F. de Waal and many other primatologists, based on the research in chimpanzees, other primates and dolphins, believe that the sense of justice, and the rules of hierarchisation and exercising of power have evolved from animal communities. Human morality, the sense of justice and respect for power are not only cultural constructs, but are rooted in those primitive, biological rules[278].

Power and ownership

Ownership is, apart from money and professional specialisation, one of the bases for economic development. Its origins can be found in primates, but only in human societies does it play the role of the key resource in regulating social relations. By ownership I mean the owning of resources and being able to dispose of them in any way one sees fit, in order to fulfil one's own will.

Research into the genesis of ownership in human societies has so far mainly covered intercultural comparative research in the field of anthropology, observations of primates, analyses of children's behaviour in the field of developmental psychology and research of evolutionary psychology and socio-biology. The conclusions of this research prove that ownership is based on biological foundations and that its origins can be traced back to primates, although it is not an 'ownership instinct', as it also has diverse cultural forms. Among the cultural universals, one can only say that ownership is present in all studied societies and is related to power, i.e. the rules of social stratification.

---

277 T. Hobbes, *The Matter, Forme and Power of a Common Wealth Ecclesiasticall and Civil*, http://archive.org/stream/hobbessleviathan00hobbuoft#page/n3/mode/2up

278 F. de Waal, *Primates and Philosophers. How Morality Evolved*, Princeton University Press, Princeton, Oxford 2006; F. de Wall, *Good Natured...*, op. cit., pp. 161-162.

Evolutionary psychologists link the beginnings of ownership to power and the jealousy of sexual partners, transferred onto objects[279]. Sexual jealousy is rooted in biology through the mechanism of protecting one's own genetic pool. It is especially strong in species which display the tendency to monogamy.

The spreading of the norms of ownership in communities of hominids could have first been based on imitation and learning, and has now become a stable evolutionary strategy[280]. Among many other theories concerning the beginnings of ownership, one could mention the symbolic complementation concept and the hypothesis of the "extended self"[281].

Summary

The neoevolutionary approach offers interesting research into power, which is derived mostly from primatology, as well as psychology and evolutionary anthropology. Research shows that power, although subject to modifications under the influence of cultural factors, is deeply rooted in evolutionary sources. In this sense, power occupies an important position in the human system of needs and is the basis for the development of many other social processes, such as war, aggressive behaviour, relations between the sexes, ownership and leadership.

On the one hand, power is subject to rational control in the case of planned activities, but on the other, due to being rooted in relatively "evolutionarily old and deep" structures of the brain, it is a highly emotional and intuitive sphere. The rapid development of civilisation and transfer of the power patterns from the Pleistocene hunter-gatherer communities onto modern and historic societies caused a number of tensions. Modern wars are driven by similar individual and group emotions as in primitive communities, but their consequences – due to technological development – are immeasurably more destructive than they were several dozen thousand years ago. Collectively induced aggression in mass societies gives rise to similar dangers. Evolutionary research could be used to interpret the sources of behaviour related to power and to suggest ways to diminish certain risks.

---

279 A. Campbell, *A Few Good Men...*, op. cit.

280 A.N. Meltzoff, W. Prinz, "The Imitative Mind: Development, Evolution and Brain Bases", *Cambridge Studies in Cognitive Perceptual Development*, Cambridge University Press, Cambridge 2002, vol. 6.

281 J.L. Pierce, T. Kostova, K.T. Dirks, "The State of Psychological Ownership: Integrating and Extending a Century of Research", *Review of General Psychology* 2003, no. 7, pp. 84-107.

The processes of power distribution translates into the creation of social structure, which is constructive for all types of society. This is why research and reflections on power are and will be developed by many different disciplines of science. However, the neoevolutionary current allows for integration of the results of research into the genesis of power and its original features. The cultural variability of power is based on biological foundations and rarely develops as a result of antinomy. From the point of view of management sciences, there should be a theory of power that would allow for the modelling of processes related to management[282].

282 Ł. Sułkowski, *Universal Sources of Hierarchy and Power from the Perspective of Neo-evolutionism*, "Journal of Intercultural Management", Vol 1, Nr 2, 2009.

Chapter 9
Leaders as evolutionary legacy

Introduction

The evolutionist perspective sheds new light on many social processes, that are key to the point of view of organisation and management[283]. An important, although methodologically difficult problem of management is leadership. Based on the evidence drawn from primatological and palaeo-anthropological research, one can assume that leadership was one of the more important social processes of our ancient ancestors, integrating the primeval communities of hominids, anthropoids and primitive people[284]. However, due to the indirect character of conclusions and little evidence, it is very difficult to present a verified theory of the evolution of leadership.

The aim of this chapter is to analyse the shape of model of leadership that emerges from evolutionary research. What is especially interesting is the possibility of complementing the leadership concept with research into the traces of the development of mankind, created within the fields of management, sociology and psychology.

Heritage of leadership

Leadership is part of the symbolic heritage of mankind, and can be analysed in primitive societies only based on anthropological research and the consequences of their actions. It is very difficult to find empirical data concerning leadership, and it requires rather indirect conclusions. It looks like hypothetical analyses and speculations, which – in the field of evolutionism – S.J. Gould called "just so stories"[285]. However, it seems that despite limited accuracy and reliability of the data, it is worth carrying out an evolutionary analysis of the leadership

---

283 J. Barkow, *Darwin, Sex and Status: Biological Approaches to Mind and Culture*, University of Toronto Press, Toronto 1989.

284 M. van Vugt, "Evolutionary Origins of Leadership and Followership", *Personality and Social Psychology Review* 2006, no. 10, pp. 354-371; N.A. Chagnon, "Life Histories, Blood Revenge, and Warfare in a Tribal Population", *Science* 1988, vol. 239, pp. 985-992; J. Tooby, L. Cosmides, *The Evolution of War and its Cognitive Foundations*, Institute for Evolutionary Studies Technical Report 1988, no. 88, pp. 1-15.

285 S.J. Gould, http://prelectur.stanford.edu/lecturers/gould/excerpts/index.html, March 2009.

phenomenon, mostly because it is a part of the neoevolutionary paradigm, being the basis for the interpretation of the whole human behaviour. Using this anthropological data and neoevolutionary models, one can put forward a neoevolutionary hypothesis concerning the emergence of leadership.

The most important issues to be considered while creating the neoevolutionary model of leadership include:

- Reasons for the appearance of leaders in primitive groups,
- The social role and specificity of the leader's power,
- Attributes of a leader,
- Dynamics between a social group and its leader.

In primitive groups, leadership emerges spontaneously for biological and functional reasons. From the biological point of view, dominance, as well as holding power and leadership in a group, are phenomena characteristic only of people[286]. Hierarchy and the fight for dominance can be also found in the world of animals[287]. These are among the most important manifestations of natural and sexual selection, as the dominant individuals usually maximise their chances for survival and reproduction. However, in many species' cases, the dominant could not be called leaders. Animal leaders have emerged only in species that have the herd instinct, which is most sophisticated in social animals with the most developed brain, such as apes[288].

In the functional sense, the emergence of a leader in a group increases the chances for survival and reproduction of a larger number of its members. In this case, leadership is a social mechanism based on the natural selection of individuals, and not whole groups[289]. The choosing of a leader in primeval groups, i.e. clans including several dozen members who are often kin, clearly increases the members' chances for reproduction of their own genes. Naturally, the key unsolved problems here are the characteristics of leadership in such groups. Were they autocratic or participative? Were they of a transactional or transformational character? How permanent was the role of the leader? Was it more frequently men or women who became leaders?

---

286 F. de Waal, *Chimpanzee Politics: Sex and Power among Apes*, The Johns Hopkins University Press, Baltimore 1982.

287 V.B. Dröscher, *Die Welt, in der die Tiere leben*.,Rasch und Röhring, Hamburg 1991, pp. 86-114.

288 F. de Waal, *Chimpanzee Politics...*, op. cit.

289 R.L. Trivers, *Social Evolution*, The Benjamin/Cummings Publishing Company, Inc., California 1985.

The social role of a leader is related to building authority and holding permanent power in a group. The classical concept of power legitimisation by Weber points to three possible sources of authority, which were probably reflected in primitive groups: rational, traditional and charismatic. In the case of primeval communities, the rational mechanism could mean subordination to the individual who offered the group members the best chances for development. These could include life experience, physical fitness, skilful social communication and the ability to cooperate. Traditional premises are mostly related to inheriting the position of leader. The first historic traces of the Sumerians and Egyptians clearly indicate that traditional power legitimisation dominated in larger communities. This kind of legitimisation must probably also have been rooted in smaller groups, which dominated the development of mankind for many millennia.

The traditional legitimisation of the leader's power is probably related to religious factors, while charisma is a certain combination of psycho-sociological features, which help gain authority – charismatic people could combine physical fitness and social intelligence. Probably the reputation of the most effective hunter and the ability to win over supporters, cooperate and form coalitions were the elements of leadership traits. No one knows whether they were in any way related to seniority and life experience, or if the dominant factor really was physical fitness. However, as modern research shows, people with better physical characteristics (e.g. a certain height, deep voice etc) are more often perceived as effective leaders.

A certain combination of personality traits makes it easier to achieve the position of the leader. This observation is in accordance with the assumption of the charismatic leadership concept, but is of a stochastic character. Not all leaders posses the same traits, while leadership itself is largely dependent on situational factors. Furthermore, there is no agreement as to the characteristics of these leadership traits.

R.D. Mann, based on conducted research, made the following list:
1. Intelligence,
2. Masculinity,
3. Adjustment,
4. Dominance,
5. Extraversion,
6. Conservatism[290].

290 R.D. Mann, "A Review of the Relationships between Personality and Performance in Small Groups", *Psychological Bulletin* 1959, no. 56, pp. 241-270.

S. Kirkpatrick and E.A. Locke proposed five traits that allow leaders to be distinguished from non-leaders:

1. Motivation,
2. Drive,
3. Integrity,
4. Confidence,
5. Task knowledge[291].

R.G. Lord, C.L. DeVader and G.M. Alliger presented a very limited list of predispositions, which includes:

1. Intelligence,
2. Masculinity,
3. Dominance[292].

Another analysis, which takes into consideration evolutionary conditions, points to the striving for domination combined with social intelligence, which is extraversion and skills in communication and cooperation[293].

The essence of leadership lies not only in the leaders themselves, but mostly in their relations with their subordinates. A rich theory concerning the formation of ties between leaders and their supporters shows that there are numerous factors influencing the quality of these relations, such as the maturity of group members, the complexity of tasks, the types of bonuses, the speed of feedback, the types of exchanges they have, and many others[294]. However, trying to simplify the picture of these relations in neoevolutionary terms, we could say that the leader, as part of their relations with their subordinates, creates the social order and makes the key decisions. Most challenges faced by people in primeval groups were of a social character, as they concerned hunting, gathering food, building shelters or protection against external attacks. This provided space for the development of the social role of a leader who coordinated group activities, was the guarantor of

291 S. Kirkpatrick, E.A. Locke, "Leadership: Do Traits Matter?", *Academy of Management Executive* 1991, no. 5(2), pp. 48-60.

292 R.G. Lord, C.L. DeVader, G.M. Alliger, "A Meta-Analysis of the Relation between Personality Traits and Leadership Perceptions: An Application of Validity Generalization Procedures", *Journal of Applied Psychology* 1986, no. 71, pp. 402-410.

293 J. Hogan, B.I. Holland, "Using Theory to Evaluate Personality and Job-Performance Relations", *Journal of Applied Psychology* 2003, no. 88, pp. 100-112; M. van Vugt, "Evolutionary Origins...", op. cit.

294 Cf. P. Hersey, K.H. Blanchard, D.E. Johnson, *Management of Organizational Behaviour: Leading Human Resources*, Prentice Hall, New York 2007; V.H. Vroom, P.W. Yetton, *Leadership and Decision-Making*, University of Pittsburgh Press, Pittsburgh 1973.

social order and distributed goods fairly. Furthermore, it solved a number of the problems of the group, related to, for example, providing greater security to its members or reducing and punishing social idleness ('freeriding')[295].

Leadership in human groups

The neoevolutionary concept of leadership explains how it developed on biological grounds. In human societies, leadership took forms previously unknown among animals. One could point to a number of differences between leadership in the world of animals and in the world of people:

- Symbolic forms of leadership,
- Leadership in a hierarchical structure,
- Leadership in a formal structure,
- Leadership in a large social group,
- Transformational leadership.

The birth of material and symbolic culture contributed to a change in the essence of power and leadership in primitive groups. The emergence and development of language, which allowed us to describe reality in a symbolic way and to transmit abstract ideas amongst people, had a profound influence on leadership processes which – similarly to power and hierarchy – started to become symbolic. The leader became the holder of authority and power, located at the top of the social hierarchy, which was reflected in the languages, rituals, myths, stories and taboos of different peoples. The oldest written materials, coming out from stories and narrations, such as *The Epic of Gilgamesh*, *The Iliad* or the Bible, glorify the actions of leaders and, at the same time, emphasise that they were anointed by the gods. As larger social groups developed, which led to the formation of ancient countries, the leaders began to exercise hierarchical, formal and symbolic control over large groups of people living in a given territory. The formation of institutionalised hierarchical structures leads to the development of multi-layered leadership. As specialisations deepen, the roles of religious, state, military and political leaders separate. Different forms of exercising power develop, based on the formalisation that substitutes leadership, such as state bureaucracy or military hierarchy[296].

---

295 B.M. Knauft, "Reconsidering Violence in Simple Human Societies: Homicide among the Gebusi of New Guinea", *Current Anthropology* 1987, no. 28, pp. 457-499.

296 Cf. A.W. Johnson, T. Earle, *The Evolution of Human Societies: From Foraging Group to Agrarian State*, Stanford University Press, Stanford 1987.

A characteristic feature of leadership in social groups of *Homo sapiens* is the dichotomy between transactional leadership and transformational leadership. This division was proposed in 1978 by M. Burns[297]. Transactional leadership is based on a proposal or promise to exchange symbolic or material goods with subordinates in return for the performance of specific tasks. Transformational leadership consists in developing a new quality of social relations, as a result of the common efforts of the leader and their supporters. Transformational leaders aim at changing values and implementing their vision through the emotional and cognitive involvement of their supporters. In this sense, animal leaders are always of transactional character, while 'true' leadership in the human world is transformational.

Summary

The neoevolutionary concept of leadership is still at the initial stages of development. Thanks to this concept, we can explain the processes behind the exercising of power based on the assumption that there is a biological continuity and concordance with the mechanisms of natural and sexual selection. At the same time, this is a concept that gives rise to numerous questions, most of which are unanswered. It is a kind of cognitive framework, which places leadership in the broader evolutionary concept of human behaviour and allows diagnosis and forecasting of human behaviour in accordance with evolutionary rules. It is also possible to undertake empirical research, in order to test the hypotheses of neoevolutionary leadership.

A critical look at the neoevolutionary concept of leadership raises questions about its cognitive value. If we focus only on the emergence of the symbolic level of leadership in the case of social groups of people, then the continuity of deliberations concerning power, hierarchy and leadership on the animal level is broken. However, it seems that the origins of human nature, which influence social processes such as leadership, are deeply rooted in biology. Thus, many explanations related to power holding, management and hierarchy will be entangled in the evolution and functioning of *Homo sapiens* in primitive groups. This aspect of the explanations of organisational and psychological processes has usually been ignored by the social sciences.

Summing up the essence of the neoevolutionary concept of leadership, it is worth pointing to several of its key ideas:

297 M. Burns, *Leadership*, Harper & Row, New York 1978.

1. Leadership is rooted in the biological nature of people who are social beings, having the most developed cognitive system. This inevitably leads to the development of group complexity and the appearance of problems concerning the emergence of comprehensive power structures and multi-layered hierarchy.
2. Leadership is beneficial to group members, as it contributes to the social order and supports the coordination of team activities, and is beneficial to leaders as it provides them with material benefits, reproductive advantages and symbolic bonuses.
3. Leadership resembles a social game, which includes tensions between the leader's attempts to seize autocratic power and the group's attempts to participate; between the interests of an individual and the interests of the group (individual sacrifice), as well as between the rivalry and cooperation of the group members.
4. Leadership has become one of the key social mechanisms, making it possible to create large and complex social groups, such as societies and states.
5. Leaders become the source of identification for their supporters. They are the symbols of the group, unifying it and building their group identity from it. This distinguishes the team members from their surroundings.

Chapter 10
Evolution and strategic thinking

Introduction

The aim of this chapter is to analyse the mechanisms of thinking and strategic activities that are rooted in evolution. This is an attempt to apply the neoevolutionary paradigm to the description of processes that are the subject of, for example, management studies.

The analysis of strategic management from the neoevolutionary perspective most of all requires answering the question of what it means to think strategically. It seems that one can distinguish only a few fundamental features of strategic thinking:

1. Strategy is future-oriented and combines plans with their implementation[298],
2. Strategy is a social and organisational phenomenon[299],
3. Strategy is playing with resources with the aim to achieve success[300],
4. Strategy is the feedback between cooperation and competition[301],
5. Strategy is based on entrepreneurship and leadership[302].

Such characteristics do not convey the whole complexity of strategy, but make it possible to find natural, evolutionary sources of strategic thinking and actions. Thus, being aware of the emergence of the business level and the specificity of companies' strategies, one can also see the continuity in the development of organisational processes.

---

298 Cf. B. Banerjee, M. Browne, L. Fulop, S. Lilley, S. Linsted, "Managing Strategically" in: *Management and Organization: A Critical Text*, S. Linstead, S. Lilley (eds.), Palgrave Macmillan, New York 2004, pp. 498-505.

299 Cf. D. Barry, M. Elmes, "Strategy Retold: Toward a Narrative View of Strategic Discourse", *Academy of Management Review* 1997, no. 22, pp. 429-452.

300 Cf. D.J. Collis, C.A. Montgomery, *Corporate Strategy, Resources and Scope of the Firm*, McGraw Hill, New York 1997.

301 Cf. S.D. Hunt, R.M. Morgan, "The Comparative Theory of Competition", *Journal of Marketing* 1995, no. 59.

302 Cf. M.A. Hitt, R.D. Ireland, S.M. Camp, D.L. Sexton (eds.), *Strategic Entrepreneurship. Creating a New Mindset*, Blackwell, Oxford 2002.

Planning

Plan-making, i.e. predicting the future in a conscious way and then shaping it, is an evolutionary mechanism that helps individuals survive in changeable social and natural conditions. The evolutionary process has equipped the human mind with cognitive mechanisms which allow for predicting and planning the future[303]. This feature is not characteristic only of the human mind; what is important is how well it is developed. Many primates are able to recognise their identity and other individuals, show empathy and predict changes in their environment, as well as to influence them by their own actions[304].

As a process, plan-making is determined by our cognitive resources, rooted in the past of mankind. Unlike computers, we plan a very limited number of variants and tend to extrapolate tendencies from the past, we use heuristics, and the key role in our process of plan-making is played by emotions and intuition[305].

Social and organisational aspects of strategy

Homo sapiens is a social species. Most challenges related to survival and reproduction arise within social groups. The key organisational problems concerning hierarchy, power, communication between individuals, as well as competition and cooperation, are also problems rooted in 'human nature'[306]. The situation is similar in the case of strategy, i.e. making plans and implementing them. Millions of years of life in primeval communities made the representatives of our species, and previously of their ancestors, able to plan group and individual actions. Although the pressure of natural selection refers to the gene pool and individuals, apart from kinship (genetic) ties, group ties have evolved, which are based on cooperation (group identity, friendship ties, neighbourhood ties)[307].

---

303 Cf. D. Sperber, "The Modularity of Thought and the Epidemiology of Representations" in: *Mapping the Mind*, L. Hirshfeld, R. Gelman (eds.), Cambridge University Press, Cambridge 1994, pp. 39-67.

304 D.L. Cheney, R.M. Seyfarth, *How Monkeys See the World: Inside the Mind of Another Species*, University of Chicago Press, Chicago 1990.

305 D. Casacuberta, *La Mente Humana*, Grupo Oceano, 2002

306 S. Pinker, *The Blank Slate: The Modern Denial of Human Nature*, Viking Press, 2002, pp. 599-617.

307 P. Seabright, *The Company of Strangers. A Natural History of Economic Life*, Princeton University Press, Princeton-Oxford 2004.

There has been positive feedback between the development of plan-making and the process of social communication. Predicting the future is a function founded on experience. Social communication, based on a common language, allows accumulation of the experiences and knowledge of many generations[308]. The evolution of language, leading to the increase in its complexity and precision in describing reality, enabled the development of plan-making using abstract notions (e.g. numbers)[309]. Another social feature of our cognitive system, allowing for planning of actions related to other people, is the 'intuitive mind theory', based on empathy[310]. This is the ability to predict the behaviour, intentions and attitudes of other people, and makes it possible to identify with them, forming intentionality[311]. This theory of the intuitive mind, the origins of which have been found in chimpanzees, is the prerequisite for making effective action plans in a social environment[312].

Modern management theories are of a social character, mostly due to a group's surroundings (for example, the interested parties), resources and stakes in the social game[313]. The obvious measures of organisational success and development, then, are socially relative. Money, profit or market share are abstract social measures of the success of organisations and their members, being the source of their satisfaction. Therefore, the resources of organisations, such as knowledge, competence, symbolic brand value or even financial resources, are also a social phenomena, which make sense only when people recognise them and believe in them.

Social evolutionary game

The notion of strategy is influenced by two very popular metaphors: game and war. Applying game theory to the business of making decisions and organising,

308 T.W. Deacon, *The Symbolic Species. The Co-evolution of Language and the Brain*, W.W. Norton & Company, New York 1997, pp. 321-373.

309 D. Bickerton, *Language and Species*, University of Chicago Press, Chicago 1990.

310 H.M. Wellman, *The Child's Theory of Mind*, MIT press, Cambridge Mass. 1990.

311 A. Gopnik, "How We Know Our Own Minds: the Illusion of First-person Knowledge and Intentionality", *Behavioral and Brain Sciences* 1993, no. 16, pp. 29-113.

312 F. de Waal, *Good Natured. The Origins of Right and Wrong in Humans and Other Animals*, Harvard University Press, Cambridge Mass.-London 1996, pp. 66-70.

313 K. Weick, "Substitutes for Corporate Strategy" in: *The Competitive Challenge, Strategies for Industrial Innovation and Renewal*, D.J. Teece, E. Ballinger (eds.), Harper and Row, Cambridge Mass. 1987, pp. 22-33.

allows analysis of the rational variants of action[314]. Social games relate to situations which include a sequence of actions undertaken by social actors who own resources and try to be successful. Stakes in a social game being the object of strategy have their origin in primitive evolutionary stakes that were related to individual survival and reproductive success[315]. Individuals have to avoid predators, parasites and other dangerous organisms, which have led to the evolution of stress responses, as well as fear and phobias related to different animals[316]. Individual survival depends mostly on having food, as well as shelter, weapons and tools. Thus, one could formulate a hypothesis that the need to possess and own is rooted in human nature.

As people perceive functioning in time (they predict and make plans), there is a pressure on social institutions to evolve towards mechanisms securing one's possessions (ownership). At the same time, individuals who have few possessions press for a change in the rules of the game, which would allow them to increase the number of their possessions. This mechanism of social inequality, inherent in the rules of the social game, is also related to power holding. Power and hierarchy, which emerge in a natural way, allow maintenance of order in a social group, and constitute the rules of group organisation and the distribution of common goods[317]. Reproductive success consists in handing down as large a gene pool as possible to one's descendants. The reproductive instinct is a universal explanation of the needs for having children, kin ties, parenthood, searching for a partner and love[318]. Social game stakes in the form of reproductive success are an obvious reflection of values related to family and children, while less obviously they are also linked with the striving for power, prestige and success[319].

---

314 J. von Neumann, I. Morgenstern, *Theory of Games and Economic Behavior*, Princeton University Press, Princeton-Oxford 2004, p. 46.

315 A. Zahavi, A. Zahavi, *The Handicap Principle: A Missing Piece of Darwin's Puzzle*, Oxford University Press, Oxford 1997; D.M. Buss, *Evolutionary Psychology. The New Science of the Mind*, Pearson, Boston 2008, pp. 72-102.

316 H.S. Bracha, "Freeze, Flight, Fight, Fright, Faint: Adaptionist Perspectives on the Acute Stress Response Spectrum", *CNS Spectrum* 2004, no. 9, pp. 679-685; I. Marks, *Fears, Phobias, and Rituals: Panic, Anxiety, and Their Disorders*, Oxford University Press, New York 1987.

317 D. Cummins, "Domination, Status, and Social Hierarchies" in: *The Handbook of Evolutionary Psychology*, D.M. Buss (ed.), Wiley, New York 2005, pp. 676-697.

318 R. Dawkins, *The Selfish Gene*, Oxford University Press, Oxford 1976.

319 D.T. Kenrick, S.L. Neuberg, K.L. Zierk, J.M. Krones, "Evolution and Social Cognition: Contrast Effects as a Function of Sex, Dominance, and Physical Attractiveness", *Personality and Social Psychology Bulletin* 1994, no. 20, pp. 210-217.

Social groups have developed their organisational skills as part of the evolutionary process, although as an emergent system they also have some unique features that cannot be found on the biological level. Organisational games concern not only individuals from a social group, but most of all whole organisations, understood as coalitions of individuals bound by social ties and identifying with one another. The stakes in the game for organisational success are social and relative, but usually measurable. Strategic management focuses on modelling the strategic games of the organisation and looking for their optimum variants.

Feedback between competition and cooperation

In the case of social species, the evolutionary success of individuals is based on the feedback between competition and cooperation, both in immediate and strategic (key and future) actions. Competition for limited resources is the basis for natural selection. However, not all individuals can be equally successful, as the evolutionary game also includes losers whose genes were supplanted by the genes of others. Still, the evolution of our species is not a zero-sum game. The development of cooperation related to communication and social ties has contributed to the achievement of success by countless individuals who have cooperated in a social group[320]. Observation of chimpanzees and bonobos show that the highest positions in the hierarchy are often occupied by the individuals who are most socially adept (those good at forming coalitions), even though they may not be the strongest, and that the origins of morality can already be found in the behaviour of apes[321].

In the course of evolution, the human mind has been equipped with very subtle modules stimulating cooperation between individuals. An example of this are the modules responsible for social communication, intuitive mind theory, and finding and punishing fraudsters and free-riders[322]. Cooperation between individuals is a strategy assuring success only when the most individuals in the group are involved in it. If the group begins to be dominated by exploratory

---

320 H. Gintis, S. Bowles, R. Bozd, E. Fher, "Explaining Altruistic Behavior in Humans" in: R.I.M. Dunbar, L. Barrett, *Evolutionary Psychology*, Oxford University Press, New York 2007; E. Wyman, M. Tomasello, "The Ontogenetic Origins of Human Cooperation" in R.I.M. Dunbar, L. Barrett, *Evolutionary Psychology*, Oxford University Press, New York 2007.

321 F. de Waal, *Primates and Philosophers. How Morality Evolved*, Princeton University Press, Princeton-Oxford 2006, pp. 3-58.

322 L. Barrett, R. Dunbar, J. Lycett, *Human Evolutionary Psychology*, Palgrave Macmillan, New York 2002, pp. 67-72, 296-308.

behaviour, which does not include positive mutuality, i.e. by non-cooperative behaviour, then cooperation no longer makes sense and all individuals lose. In the case of many primates, evolution has led to the protection and maintenance of cooperation through the module enabling the identification and punishment of the lack of mutuality (social fraud)[323]. Recognition of individuals and social communication allow for the dissemination of negative knowledge about non-cooperative individuals (e.g. gossips). Non-cooperative individuals are subject to sanctions in the form of, for example, ostracism.

Competition, conflicts for resources, violence and war also have biological origins. In the case of social species, competition and conflicts can be escalated to fights between coalitions within the group, sometimes leading to the division of the social group into two hostile teams. In the case of chimpanzees, group conflicts and wars between groups of individuals have been observed[324], therefore even xenophobia or hostility towards strangers and others are built on evolutionary foundations. War seems to be one of the most complex human group activities, requiring effective planning and coordination of group actions. As a matter of fact, the notion of strategy was initially inseparably related to war.

Strategic management is not free of metaphors of game and war. On the one hand, organisational strategy is linked with cooperation between different market units (including competitors), and on the other, with market competition for limited resources. Competition is considered to be the universal mechanism of the improvement of the market and units functioning within it, the counterpart of which can be natural selection aimed at better adjustment to the environment. However, one has to remember that market competition is based on the mechanism of learning and decision-making, while natural selection is based on a thoroughly random mechanism of mutation.

Competition plays the key role in the theory of strategic management, both in the case of the positional school, and in the case of the evolutionary or resource school. Competition and cooperation are understood in two ways. On the one hand, they are treated as processes controlled by decision-makers, but on the other, as social processes which are to a large extent indeterministic and form a kind of open social game. M.E. Porter, who takes the rationalistic an mostly deterministic view, openly uses the notion of 'competition strategies', which indicates the activity of economic units in the competition and

---

323 M.E. Price, L. Cosmides, J. Tooby, "Punitive Sentiment as an Anti-free Rider Psychological Device", *Evolution and Human Behaviour* 2002, no. 23, pp. 203-231.

324 J. Goodall, *Through a Window: My Thirty Years with the Chimpanzees of Gombe*, Houghton Mifflin, Boston 1990.

cooperation sector[325]. H. Mintzberg distances himself from the position, which assumes only an aware, fully controlled and almost algorithmic implementation of strategies by management, and favours an open social process that resembles learning (crafting strategy)[326]. K. Weick, criticising the planning attitude towards strategy, point to the possibility of managing opportunities in a turbulent environment[327].

Strategy based on entrepreneurship and leadership

In a social group, the combination of entrepreneurship and leadership is characteristic of mankind. Entrepreneurship is related to the ability to cope with new situations thanks to planning and implementing creative actions that enable achievement of success. Such understanding of entrepreneurship usually concerns social actions, which includes the presence of a leader. Thus, there is a clear correlation between entrepreneurship and leadership. In primeval groups – similarly to modern groups – enterprising individuals displayed creative thinking, ambition, the ability to cooperate and communicate, and the need to exercise power (dominance)[328]. Such composition of features can be treated as the essence of an 'ideal' leader, although using the theory of leadership, one could point to significant limitations in the concept of 'leadership traits'[329]. As numerous paleontological studies show, the spread of *Homo sapiens*, and previously of *Homo erectus* and *Homo Neanderthalis*, all over the Earth, is a consequence of group migrations. Increasing competition in Africa and changing climatic conditions caused groups, probably through enterprising leaders, to travel to Europe, Asia, the Americas and Australia[330]. The beginnings of the development of cultures that are related to the creation of tools, languages, beliefs, religion and art are wrapped in mystery due to their symbolic character. However, one can assume that changes and better adaptation to

325 M.E. Porter, *Competitive Strategy: Techniques for Analyzing Industry and Competitors*, Free Press, New York 1980.

326 H. Mintzberg, "Crafting Strategy", *Harvard Business Review* 1987, no. 7-8, pp. 67-81.

327 K. Weick, "Substitutes for Corporate Strategy" in: *The Competitive Challenge*, D. Teece (ed.), Ballinger, Cambridge 1987.

328 R.M. Stogdill, "Historical Trends in Leadership Theory and Research", *Journal of Contemporary Business* 1974, no. 3, pp. 1-17.

329 C.C. Manz, H.P. Sims Jr, "Becoming a Superleader" in: *Classic Readings in Self-Managing Teamworks*, R. Glasser (ed.), King of Prussia, Organisational Design and Development Inc., 1992.

330 C. Zimmer, *Smithsonian Guide to Human Origins*, HarperCollins Smithsonian Books, Toronto 2005, pp. 60-143.

variable conditions in different parts of the globe were made possible thanks to human entrepreneurship related to leadership[331].

"Entrepreneurship based on strategic orientation towards development, willingness to undertake moderate risk, toleration of the unspecified, learning from one's mistakes, creativity, innovation and renewal, is undoubtedly a significant complement to strategic planning"[332]. On the other hand, in the course of evolution and cultural changes, leadership – although biologically based on the need to dominate – has gained the features of entrepreneurial activities of a group leader. The emergence of enterprising leaders has allowed for the organisation and coordination of group activities which – through the processes of social communication – have led to the birth and development of culture. Thus, it is clear that although entrepreneurship and leadership are separate processes, they have been strongly intertwined in the course of the evolution of mankind. The result of this feedback is the strategic thinking of the 'third chimpanzee'[333].

Summary

The presented analysis of the evolutionary basis of human strategic thinking is of an interdisciplinary character, and combines theories developed by biology and evolutionary socio-biology with the concepts of management and theory of organization. It might seem that such a research field is too blurred and limits the possibility of conducting studies and making theoretical generalisations. However, as the experience of evolutionary economics shows, such an alliance between natural and social sciences may be very creative[334]. First of all, it constitutes a broad neoevolutionary paradigm which can be used in all research fields concerning analyses of human behaviour, i.e. being the subject of sociology, psychology, economics and management, as well as anthropology

---

331 R. Boyd, P.J. Richerson, *The Origin and Evolution of Cultures*, Oxford University Press, New York 2004.

332 M. Bratnicki, "Renta przedsiębiorczości w statycznych i dynamicznych otoczeniach" in: *Przedsiębiorczy menedżer w przedsiębiorczej organizacji*, J. Antoszkiewicz (ed.), SGH, Warszawa 2007, p. 67.

333 J. Diamond, *The Third Chimpanzee. The Evolution and Future of Human Animal*, Harper, New York 1992.

334 C. Herrmann-Pillath, "On the Ontological Foundations of Evolutionary Economics", *Evolutionary Economics. Program and Scope*, K. Dopfer (ed.), Kluwer Academic Publishers, Boston 2001, pp. 89-139; H. Simon, "Darwinism, Altruism and Economics" in: *The Evolutionary Foundations of Economics*, K. Dopfer (ed.), Cambridge University Press, New York 2005, pp. 89-104.

and biology[335]. Moreover, it allows for the transfer of theories and research methods between different disciplines, and verification of the results.

Strategic management is a sub-discipline of management sciences, aimed at answering the questions concerning making key decisions in organisations. It seems that finding answers to such questions is impossible without a reference to research into human behaviour, and especially into the mechanisms of decision-making in a group[336]. The neoevolutionary paradigm may serve as a source of inspiration, although the processes of strategic management in organisations cannot be cognitively reduced merely to Neo-Darwinist explanations.

335 L. Cronk, *The Whole Complex: Culture and Evolution of Human Behavior*, Westview Press, Boulder 1999.

336 S. Wagner-Tsukamoto, *Human Nature and Organization Theory. On the Economic Approach to Institutional Organization, New Horizons in Management*, Edward Elgar Publishing Co., Cheltenham 2003, pp. 47-64.

Chapter 11

The common good and public management from the neoevolutionary perspective

Introduction

The key problem of social life is cooperation between people. Neoevolutionism shows that 'human nature' is of a social character and develops accompanied by the tension between competition for limited resources and the cooperation that sometimes allows for their better use[337]. There are numerous different types of cooperation; the sophisticated and abstract form is the concern for the 'common good' which belongs to the whole community. Today, examples of the 'common good' could be the environment, medical and social care, public education. These are the crucial areas for which diverse economic and political solutions are adopted, usually related to the attempt to find a balance between social solidarity and the pace of economic development. Discrepancies in the current political and social systems can be attributed to cultural diversity, which is mostly a result of historical changeability in the development of societies. At the same time, there is a certain area related to the universality of the 'common good' issue. Problems with the concern for the 'common good' have their biological origins in the evolutionary construction of 'human nature', so they can be analysed from the neoevolutionary perspective. The problem of 'common good' from the point of view of mankind's evolution is discussed in the further part of this chapter.

'The tragedy of the commons'

'The tragedy of the commons' is a theoretical problem described by G. Hardin[338]. Shepherds minding sheep on a common meadow face a temptation to increase their own herd, as – from the point of view of individual economic rationality – the optimum solution is to increase one's own benefits. Increasing their herds is a secret and gradual process, as the shepherds do not want to deliberately violate the unwritten social contract or destroy the ecosystem of the meadow. However, they do regularly add sheep to their herds, and therefore

337 D.M. Buss, *Evolutionary Psychology. The New Science of the Mind*, Pearson, Boston 2008, pp. 36-69.

338 G. Hardin, "The Tragedy of the Commons", *Science* 1968, no. 162, pp. 1243-1248.

destroy the pasture. 'The tragedy of the commons' is a model of a broad social mechanism which leads to overexploitation and, in consequence, the fall of the 'common good'.

'The tragedy of the commons' is not a simple consequence of selfishness and economic rationality, but a much more complex problem related to the evolutionary sources of human behaviour. Analysing the situation of the shepherds, we could point to several assumptions about the basis for their behaviour. First of all, one of the shepherds wants to increase his benefits above the average, which means that there is an individual who has 'Machiavellian intelligence'. Second of all, the shepherds want to maintain the social order and conceal the fact of increasing their herds. Third of all, many communities develop mechanisms of protection against wasteful exploitation. These are based on social norms and sanctions imposed on individuals who break the social contract concerning fair distribution of resources, and some communities even create and maintain special social roles of 'guardians of public order', whose task is to find and punish fraudsters.

Many economists have deliberated upon the issue of the 'common good', coming up with solutions which on the one hand are aimed at its severe limitation or liquidation (including a proposal to 'privatise' rivers), and on the other, suggest the creation of effective protection mechanisms[339].

It seems that it is impossible to thoroughly eliminate the 'common good' from the human social world. However, this does not mean that the socialist and communist belief in the superiority of the 'common property' of production means is right. Quite the contrary, empirical research carried out by social and evolutionary psychology, and painful historical experience, prove how utopian such ideas are. Modern societies balance between different solutions concerning the protection of the 'common good'. This solutions are shaped by cultural conditions but in its core they are basing on biological foundations. It seems that the problem is the lack of understating of certain universal rules which are the underlying reason behind the 'tragedy of the commons', being the consequence of 'human nature' formed in the course of evolution[340].

---

339 *Modeling Rationality, Morality and Evolution*, P.A. Danielson (ed.), Oxford University Press, New York 1998, http://www.questia.com/PM.qst?a=o&d=80353474, March 25th, 2009.

340 P.J. Richerson, R.B.B. Paciotti, "An Evolutionary Theory of Commons Management", May 30th 2001, chapter intended for *Institutions for Managing the Commons*, National Research Council, Internet.

Evolutionary heritage

Neoevolutionism explain the reasons for the culturally universal mechanism of the 'tragedy of the commons'. People have the ownership instinct and strive to maximise their chances for survival and reproduction[341], which leads to excessive exploitation of goods owned by the community. Collective ownership often means not only the lack of a competitive mechanism, but also an inevitable degradation of the common good.

Analysing the origins of the 'tragedy of the commons', one has to go far back into our evolutionary past, to the time of the formation of the hereditary mental mechanisms which were the basis for a relatively flexible – but not exceeding evolutionary boundaries – human nature. Hunter-gatherer communities were the dominant form of human organisation for hundreds of thousands of years, if we take into consideration the hominids who share our genetic legacy. Groups of several dozen to about 150 individuals were the natural cradle of mankind. The key instincts of these groups were the reproduction of one's own genetic pool, and individual survival. Individuals cooperated within their families and the whole community in group hunting, sharing prey, and mutual support, and this was probably the time when strong mutuality and ownership instincts were developed. Hunter-gatherer societies possessed few items, but from the point of view of survival, they were incredibly valuable. Weapons and basic tools, as well as clothes, allowed individuals to survive. The temptation to steal objects and social sanctions for theft appeared probably also appeared at that time too.

Hunter-gatherer communities exploited common resources (e.g. forests), protecting their territories against the interference of other clans. However, the issue of 'common good' gained key importance only when hunter-gatherer societies began transforming into settled, agricultural communities. The development of farming and animal breeding took a relatively short time from the evolutionary perspective, so the old pattern of exploitation and division of goods drawn from hunter-gatherer communities was imposed on the division of new agricultural and breeding resources. Land became the property of individuals, families or whole communities and the basic source of maintenance. Conflicts over resources in the form of land or domesticated animals became common and required new social institutions. It was most likely these circumstances under which the 'tragedies of the commons' took place, as common property was exploited by the whole community until it was destroyed. As palaeoanthropological sources show, primitive agricultural communities left

341 L. Barrett, R. Dunbar, J. Lycett, *Human Evolutionary Psychology*, Palgrave Macmillan, New York 2002, pp. 22-33.

many places totally exploited, which contradicts the thesis that primeval people lived in harmony with nature. The exploitation of natural resources and the resources of one's own community is rooted in human nature, although to a certain extent it is also subject to social regulations.

However, the evolutionary explanation of the 'tragedy of the commons' is not as simple. Although it takes the form of a universal explanation independent of cultural context, the degree of consumption of the common good depends on the society, so it is culturally relative. Communitarian societies in such countries as Sweden, Denmark, Japan and South Korea reveal greater attention to the 'common good' than individualistic societies such as the USA or the United Kingdom[342]. Thus, the concern for the 'common good' is influenced by the degree of communitarianism, which is related to the social capital concept[343]. The higher the level of general trust and cooperation between the society's members, the lower the probability that the 'tragedy of the commons' will occur[344]. The universal dimension of human nature is culture-corrected, depending on the historically-formed social values and norms[345].

Another problem that should be explained is why human society on the level of hunter-gatherer communities did not solve the issue of the 'common good'. It seems natural that for millions of years people had to hunt and gather, exploiting the same resources (such as forests), but perhaps strange that they did not come up with solutions enabling a compromise. The explanation for this may be related to the lack of group selection mechanisms[346]. Selection is always located on the level of the genetic pool, so on the level of individuals, reproduction and kin. The mechanism of concern for the common good is of a secondary character and is a kind of social control and conformism imposed on individuals. Probably this was the reason for the development of a certain dynamic balance between selfish individual attempts to possess goods and reproduce one's own genetic pool, and the loyalty to the community, on condition it does not interfere with reproductive aspirations.

342 G. Hofstede, & Hofstede, G.J., *Cultures and Organizations. Software of the Mind,* (2nd edn). New York: McGraw-Hill, 2005, pp. 89-125.

343 R.D. Putnam, *Bowling Alone. The Collapse and Revival of American Community*, Simon&Schuster, New York 2000, pp. 350-365.

344 J. Henrich, R. McElreath, "Dual-Inheritance Theory: the Evolution of Human Cultural Capacities and Cultural Evolution" in: R.I.M. Dunbar, L. Barrett, *Evolutionary Psychology*, Oxford University Press, New York 2007.

345 H. Plotkin, "The power of culture" in: R.I.M. Dunbar, L. Barrett, *Evolutionary Psychology*, Oxford University Press, New York 2007.

346 R.L. Trivers, "The Evolution of Reciprocal Altruism", *Quarterly Review of Biology* 1971, no. 46, pp. 35-57.

The explanation of non-kin altruism is intuitively problematic from the neoevolutionary point of view. The interpretation of kin and family ties is based on genetic closeness and was convincingly described by W.D. Hamilton[347]. Non-kin altruism can be interpreted in two ways. Its first source is associated with genes, while the second with cooperation. Assuming that mankind developed in a primeval group, consisting mainly of kin, altruistic behaviour not only towards the closest relatives but also members of the whole clan seem rather more probable.

However, a kind of 'genetic wall' separated clans from other communities, leaving little space for altruism towards strangers. Non-kin altruism then probably stems from social cooperation mechanisms, in the case of which collaboration, task division and the exchange of goods increase the chances for survival. Thus, sharing the obtained food, helping in the face of danger and cooperating together were a kind of investment. Recognising strange individuals and mutual commitments increased the chances for survival in the future. This was the source of the natural strength of friendship, fellowship and neighbourhood ties, based on mutual commitments and transactional strategy with deferred rewards (a favour for a favour).

There is also a third possible reason for non-kin altruism, related to the structure of the human cognitive system. *Homo sapiens* have the tendency to be fascinated with ideas which may take the form of – as some authors call them – information infections. Getting infected with such ideas may lead to actions which are thoroughly impractical from the point of view of information reproduction (memes). Individuals reveal altruistic behaviour, which results from the fascination with ideology, politics or religion, paying no attention to its negative influence on their own survival.

The issue of altruism has been adopted for economics in accordance with the neoevolutionary approach by H.A. Simon[348]. Modern analyses of altruistic behaviour are carried out not only in relation to population and social behaviour, but also neurobiology, mostly through research into the function of 'mirror neurons'[349].

---

347 W.D. Hamilton, "The Genetical Evolution of Social Behaviour", *Journal of Theoretical Biology* 1964, no. 7, pp. 1-52.

348 H.A. Simon, "Darwinism, Altruism and Economics" in: *The Evolutionary Foundation of Economics*, K. Dopfer (ed.), Cambridge University Press, Cambridge 2005, pp. 102-103.

349 R.A. Barton, "Evolution of the Social Brain as a Distributed Neural System" in: R.I.M. Dunbar, L. Barrett, *Evolutionary Psychology*, Oxford University Press, New York 2007; T. Jellema, D.I. Perrett, "Neural Pathways of Social Cognition" in: R.I.M. Dunbar, L. Barrett, *Evolutionary Psychology*, Oxford University Press, New York 2007.

Another issue is that people have a tendency toward 'evolutionary cheating', or 'natural slyness'. As social experiments show, the readiness to use limited forms of deception is common, and is common to both children and adults. On the one hand, it is minimised by social sanctions and the willingness to maintain the rules of the social game, while on the other, by the feeling of hurting a specific individual. In the case of the 'tragedy of the commons', all the limitations of 'evolutionary slyness' are greatly reduced. Social sanctions are usually small, especially when violation of norms is common. Those exploiting the common good do not consciously try to destroy it, and actively maintain the binding social contract. However, there is no clear indication who is hurt when the common good is over-exploited.

'Social idleness', based on the so-called Ringelmann effect, is closely related to the 'tragedy of the commons'. M. Ringelmann carried out a social experiment, asking its participants to pull a rope in teams, and measured their group effort. Individual results were on average about 63 kg, a three-person group's result was 160 kg, while an eight-person group achieved barely 248 kg[350]. 'Social idleness' in the evolutionary sense is identical to the 'tragedy of the commons'. The strategy of the exploitation of a 'common meadow' is substituted with the strategy of reducing individual efforts in a way allowing their concealment, to avoid sanctions and not to violate the rules of the game as a whole. The syndrome of 'social idleness' is one of the key threats to team work and makes it necessary to introduce mechanisms that supervise and reward individual results and effort.

Reducing the negative effects

Bearing in mind the universalism of the basis for the 'tragedy of the commons', rooted in human nature and society, how can one try to reduce the negative effects of this phenomenon?

First of all, it is possible to develop values, norms and social patterns that cultivate concern for the 'common good'. Understanding the dilemma of the 'tragedy of the commons' and using it as a metaphor or even explanation for modern environmental problems, allows formation of coalitions of people taking care of the environment. A positive example of reducing the effect of the 'tragedy of the commons' are the global agreements banning the emission of Freon and greenhouse gases. These are based on a voluntary agreement but are

350 M. Ringelmann, "Recherches sur les Moteur Animes. Travail de l'homme", *Annales de l'Institut National Agronomique* 1913, no. 12, pp. 2-40.

accompanied by monitoring of the emissions and the possibility to impose sanctions on those countries that do not observe the contract.

The development of social capital is closely related to the level of trust between a society's members. Thanks to attempts to increase the social capital, combined with effective systems of finding, sanctioning and punishing frauds, the 'social good' is less exposed to overexploitation by individuals who have 'Machiavellian intelligence' and other community members. In modern mass societies, the system of social supervision, sanctions and punishment is of an institutional character, but from the perspective of effectiveness, the key factor is its internalisation by its society's members – this is the feeling of being responsible for the 'common good' and the readiness to cultivate it diminish the syndrome of the 'tragedy of the commons'.

The last issue is the possibility to limit the areas of the 'common good' which can be more efficiently managed and developed by private owners. Privatisation and commercialisation of certain public services may successfully decrease the degradation of the resources of the 'common good'. However, it is important to minimise the negative effects of its liquidation, such as the increase in social inequality and the fall of social solidarity. It seems that in the case of many areas of social services, e.g. health care, education, public safety, culture and science, excessive limitation of the 'common good' is harmful from the point of view of the whole society.

Summary

The issue of the 'common good' is a classic example of economic, sociological or even political deliberations concerning social cooperation. However, introducing the neoevolutionary context may bring important new threads to the analysis of the 'tragedy of the commons'. People reveal a natural tendency to cooperate and compete, which has been developed in the course of evolution. This is why the structure of the social order, the aim of which is to protect and develop the 'common good', cannot negate the essence of human nature. Knowledge about our biological and evolutionary roots might help to build a social order that would decrease the problem of the 'tragedy of the commons'.

However, using this knowledge requires researchers to apply an interdisciplinary approach, building bridges between disciplines which traditionally occupy opposite positions. Examples of valuable research, combining natural and social sciences, can be found in evolutionary psychology and socio-biology. It seems that the deliberations concerning the 'common good' require assumption of a pluralist and non-orthodox position, which allows inclusion of the results of cultural research and the works of natural sciences in the analyses of human behaviour.

Chapter 12
Neoevolutionary marketing

Introduction

The aim of this chapter is to analyse the applications for the neoevolutionary current in marketing. Modern biological and social sciences draw from Darwinian theory, mostly proposing an image of human nature rooted in the evolutionary processes. Marketing is also based on research into human behaviour, so it should be able to draw significant inspiration from neoevolutionism.

Marketing is a practice-oriented discipline, allowing organisations to achieve success by getting to know and satisfying their customers' needs. However, as modern neoevolutionary research shows, all types of customer behaviour are rooted in evolution. Marketing has rarely used evolutionary interpretations of market activities, although practitioners who rely on intuition have developed heuristics that in many cases can be described as pragmatic consequences of the neoevolutionary paradigm. The originator of behavioural economics, A. Tversky, noticed that salesmen and advertising specialists make use of intuitive knowledge about cognitive illusions [351]. What are the consequences of the key assumptions of the neoevolutionary current for marketing?

Darwinism and marketing

Starting with the sphere of needs, one can find two basic evolutionary sources of human aspiration: individual survival and reproduction. These translate into a number of complex mental modules, being a kind of software aimed at satisfying these needs[352]. In primitive groups, survival depended on the ability to find food and avoid predators, and on a wider scale, it depended on group cooperation. Obtaining food is a universal pursuit which entails numerous problems in modern consumerist society. Whereas the tendency to eat excessive amounts of calorific food was a natural adjustment by primitive people, it is now

---

351 A. Tversky, D. Kahneman, "Availability: A Heuristics for Judging Frequency and Probability" in: *Judgment Under Uncertainty: Heuristics and Biases*, D. Kahneman, P. Slovic, A. Tversky (eds.), Cambridge University Press, New York 1982.

352 H.C. Barrett, R. Kurzban, "Modularity in Cognition: Framing the Debate", *Psychological Review* 2006, no. 113, pp. 628-647.

impractical in developed societies and is the reason for pathological obesity and other health problems[353]. Marketing communication often refers to the motivations behind feeding, using human attachment to appetising foods, and thus signalling their calorific value.

Another key motive of marketing communication is, obviously, sex. This stems from the reproductive urge, and although contraceptive methods have effectively limited reproduction, its motivating force – the sex drive – has remained intact. Aesthetics are rooted in human sexuality and probably related to sexual impulses. Ideals of beauty include a symmetrical body of perfect proportions, which supports reproduction and the survival of children. In many cases, the basis for human behaviour is sex, starting from the strategy of sex selection and self-presentation, through seduction, to romantic love and responsibility for one's family[354]. Sexual references in marketing are not only communication but often also products that satisfy needs. This does not only concern products related to the sex act itself, but all kinds of social needs that stimulate contact between men and women, such as entertainment.

Sexual differences also have evolutionary sources. As the research carried out by evolutionary psychologists shows, *Homo sapiens* reveal different perception and interpretation abilities dependant on gender, which probably results from the specialisation of social roles related to looking for food. Women prove to be more effective at finding details in spaces, while men have better spatial imagination[355]. In the course of evolution, women have adjusted to gathering, while the men have adjusted to hunting. Undoubtedly, there are also emotional differences related to, for example, different sexual strategies and family roles (maternity). Men are more jealous in terms of sex, which is their subconscious attempt to secure the certainty of paternity. In the case of women, statistically, the prevailing jealousy is of an emotional character, as they focus on the stability of their relationships and children's interests[356]. Women usually reveal lower levels of aggression and stronger empathy, while men tend to behave in a competitive way.

Marketers use sexual dimorphism for the purposes of segmentation and targeting in the preparation of gender-oriented marketing. Such differentiation

353 J.P.J. Prinel, S. Assanand, D.R. Lehman, "Hunger, Eating and Ill Health" in: *The Functional Mind. Readings in Evolutionary Psychology*, D.T. Kenrick, C.L. Luce (eds.), Pearson, Boston 2004, pp. 17-35.

354 B.S. Low, *Why Sex Matters: A Darwinian Look at Human Behaviour*, Princeton University Press, Princeton 2000.

355 D. Kimura, *Sex and cognition*, The MIT Press, 1999, pp. 50-74.

356 S. Cashdan, "Women's Mating Strategies", *Evolutionary Anthropology* 1996, no. 5, pp. 134-143.

can be found practically in most modern products, starting from cosmetics and clothes, through books, films and cars, to services. Marketing communication also differs depending on the gender of the group being targeted for the given items. Women's advertisements more often refer to taking care of children and strengthening emotional ties, while those aimed at men feature elements of fighting and rivalry. Though the danger of gender-related interpretations is excessive stereotyping, it is worth emphasising that the relationship between sex and behaviour is only of a statistical character and should not be used to interpret individual traits.

Another interesting commercial adjustment by marketing to human nature is the use of neoteny, i.e. the tendency to recognise children's faces and provide care based on that recognition. The culturally universal sensitivity of human perception to facial expressions is very high[357]; emotions communicated by the face are recognised from a very young age, and two dots and a line below are interpreted by most people as a face (*gestalt*). Ultimately, it's no wonder children are one of the most popular motifs used in marketing. Many modern animated films tell stories with the use of children's faces disguised as cars (*Cars*), animals (*Ice Age*) or fantasy creatures (*Shrek*). Advertisements for cleaning products often refer to the narration of an idealised family, the centre of which is occupied by a child.

Avoidance of predators is a mental module inherited by *Homo sapiens* from the ancient past and the reason for stress, involuntary aggressive responses, escape, phobias, the innate fear of the dark, and many other traits of human nature. Aversive stimuli related to the fears rooted in human nature are used in marketing communication, mostly to attract attention and fill the message with emotion. The module of avoiding predators guarantees a prompt involuntary response, as the chances for individual survival depend on the speed of the response[358]. Furthermore, an aversive stimulus entails a strong emotional response. This may be one of the reasons for the effectiveness of aggressive, negative campaigns, used for example in the American media during presidential campaigns, or advertisements from the pharmaceutical and insurance sectors, which are based on fear.

357 P. Ekman, W.V. Friesen, "Constants across Cultures in the Face and Emotion" in: *The Functional Mind. Readings in Evolutionary Psychology*, D.T. Kenrick, C.L. Luce (eds.), Pearson, Boston 2004, pp. 130-138.

358 D. Evans, O. Zarate, *Introducing Evolutionary Psychology*, Icon Book, London 2006, pp. 50-56.

Selling human nature

Analysing human nature, one can distinguish a group of features characteristic only, or mostly, of mankind. This group does not include the above mentioned needs to obtain food, avoid predators or reproduce. Also, sexual dimorphism and care for children are not features characteristic only of *Homo sapiens*. The unique features include, for example, the striving for ownership, self-awareness, creativity, communication and development of culture.

One very interesting, universal need, is the striving for ownership, which can be found in all known societies. Referring to the experience of primitive groups, ownership probably stemmed from the basic needs (e.g. obtaining food), which were closely linked to social needs – striving for a higher status, and dominance. For primeval people, and even for their predecessors (e.g. *Homo habilis*), owning tools and weapons was very important. The animals hunted and food gathered was controlled by the group members, which was the origin of ownership. As the hunter-gatherer communities developed, and after the first animals were domesticated, these animals became the subject of ownership, providing for the whole family and clan. Thus, it seems that owning goods became a measure of social prestige, at the same time providing individuals with the means for their survival.

Modern consumerist culture is based on the need to own goods. The accumulation of goods is a measure of success, and a way to provide individuals and families with security, a measure of prestige and the key mechanism of social control. Marketing refers to the need to own goods by modifying products and brands, and communication aimed at satisfying the ownership need. People often strive to own things not for functional, but prestige-related reasons, thus they exchange unworn products for new ones. Financial products, which allow accumulation and multiplication of money, are subject to intensive sales. This change only concerns the balance between the reasons for quick accumulation of money and security, and also in this case the evolutionary rule that applies, saying that a loss entails twice the emotional costs as a profit.

Homo sapiens have been evolutionarily adjusted to life in small groups of not more than 100-150 individuals[359]. Naturally, several thousand years ago larger social structures had developed, such as nations and societies, but these were a result of the development of culture and technology, not the evolutionary legacy[360]. Therefore, despite functioning in mass societies, mankind is mentally

359 R.I.M. Dunbar, "Neocortex Size as a Constraint on Group Size in Primates", *Journal of Human Evolution* 1992, no. 20, pp. 469-493.

360 P. Seabright, *The Company of Strangers. A Natural History of Economic Life*, Princeton University Press, Princeton, Oxford 2004, pp. 109-121.

adjusted to living in small groups. This is manifested in communications processes that focus on individual, personal, face-to-face communication. Communication using mass media is also aimed at individual recipients, as it appeals to individual needs. Another characteristic feature is the predilection for narration, plot and personal stories rooted in the individual mentality and social group dynamics. Generalisations and abstract thinking are far more problematic[361]. Social adjustment to living in small groups is also supported by empathy, friendship and coalitions that stimulate cooperative or altruistic behaviour[362], and is manifested in the strength of ties on the level of mass communication, for example in being moved by a film plot, which – as far as we know – is fictional, or attachment to the heroes in a favourite TV series.

Awareness and self-awareness are probably gradable states, which are properties of the mind and the whole nervous system. Animals display different degrees of awareness, just like people can function on different levels of awareness, depending on different stimuli, for example, pharmacological stimulation of the brain. Self-awareness, or the recognition of one's own individuality and sense of identity, can be found in certain primates (chimpanzees and bonobos), as well as people[363]. As a social species, people function within a tension between a group and individuality: on the one hand, they are dependent on their social position, while on the other they strive to satisfy their individual needs. Self-awareness is a source of diverse, complex, individual needs, such as the need for fulfilment and creativity. In marketing, a key role is also played by the balance between the need for individualisation and the feeling of social affiliation. People often want to be seen as individuals and, at the same time, as community members. Modern marketing, including the relative marketing trend, enhances the feeling of individualism in terms of fulfilling specific, individual needs. It also emphasises the possibility of the social expression of these needs, as the real value in the case of social species is the one recognised by others.

Creativity, innovativeness, resourcefulness and even entrepreneurship are almost synonymous notions. Human nature is flexible thanks to the fact that people as a species are equipped with flexible cognitive systems. By nature, people are curious about the world, and – although the fear of otherness and strangers is also biologically rooted – the tendency to want to get to know and

---

361 L. Cosmides, J.H. Tooby, "Cognitive Adaptations for Social Exchange" in: *The Adapted Mind*, J.H. Barkow, L. Cosmides, J.H. Tooby (eds.), Oxford University Press, Oxford 1992, pp. 163-228.

362 R. Axelrod, *The Evolution of Cooperation*, Basic Books, New York 1984.

363 F. de Waal, *Good Natured. The Origins of Right and Wrong in Humans and Other Animals*, Harvard University Press, Cambridge Mass.-London 1996.

create new things prevails in most societies. *Homo sapiens* and other hominids received an 'evolutionary bonus' for being inquisitive and creative. The discoveries that played the key role in the development of individuals and the species were tools, language, culture, agriculture, and their departure from the African cradle to take control of the globe. The media that revolutionised the species' development were language, and later on, culture[364]. Language, which has obvious coordinating functions for social species, has probably developed from a simpler form of animal communication, the main functions of which were signalling and emotive.

The feedback between the development of language, the brain and more and more complex social groups, has led to the development of culture, which has evolved based on the rules of accumulation and transfer of the symbolic works within a community. The pace of changes in social organisations, or even in the mental human 'software', increased rapidly in comparison with the pace of biological evolution based on the mechanisms of reproduction and genetic mutations. Marketing is a part of human symbolic culture. Although it refers to human biological resources and social needs, it spreads with the use of language communication and culture. The rules of spreading symbolic culture require further research. One of the hypotheses here is memetics, which points to the universal striving for the duplication of replicators, which can be both genes (evolution) and information (culture)[365]. From the marketing perspective, it seems popular to use comparisons transferred from biology to the world of information, for example: information as genes, fashion as epidemics[366], or the success of competing information as natural selection.

Summary

One can find several assumptions for developing a marketing theory which take into consideration the neoevolutionary assumption. First of all, all kinds of human behaviour are of an evolutionary origin. They can be a direct consequence of the evolutionary construction, e.g. the need to eat calorific food, but more often they have been modified, as for example the need to compete and fight, which have now gained symbolic rather than physical forms. Second of

364 K.N. Laland, "Niche Construction, Human Behavioral Ecology and Evolutionary Psychology" in: R.I.M. Dunbar, L. Barrett, *Evolutionary Psychology*, Oxford University Press, New York 2007.

365 R. Aunger, "Memes" in: R.I.M. Dunbar, L. Barrett, *Evolutionary Psychology*, Oxford University Press, New York 2007.

366 M. Gladwell, *The Tipping Point. How Little Things Can Make a Big Difference*, Little, Brown and Company, New York 2002, pp. 15-29.

all, evolutionary explanations refer to the functionality of behaviour in primitive societies, while today the same behaviour can be impractical. For example, the fact that people like alcohol may be a consequence of the search for ripe fruit, which has the highest content of sugar and ethanol, and in which the fermentation process has already started. Third of all, elements that influence human behaviour include adaptation and also indirect products, or even random effects. Under natural conditions, adaptations have evolved and supported survival or reproduction. Indirect products have accompanied functional solutions but have not carried any solutions supporting survival, so they are not functional. Neither are random effects, which can be of a changeable, individual character[367]. Marketing theory based on evolutionary assumptions can draw from the copious results of empirical studies carried out by behavioural economics, evolutionary psychology and neuroscience[368].

Analyses of research based on the neoevolutionary paradigm from the perspective of applications in marketing lead to interesting results. Most of all, they reveal that very complex patterns of human behaviour entail a coherent evolutionary concept which may explain them. Moreover, this limits the issue of cultural relativism, which makes it impossible to use similar ideas in different societies, indicating universals that are evolutionarily rooted, such as needs and emotions. An interesting consequence of the research carried out as part of the neoevolutionary approach is also the explanation of numerous types of human behaviour which are not included in the *Homo economicus* perspective. Seemingly irrational and illogical actions are often in accordance with the structure of needs and the specificity of the evolutionary construction of human nature[369]. Marketing, as a discipline based on behavioural sciences and, at the same time, strongly linked to market practices, has gradually discovered the heuristics that allow it to effectively influence people.

---

367 D.M. Buss, *Evolutionary Psychology. The New Science of the Mind*, Pearson, Boston 2008, pp. 39-40.

368 M. Shermer, *The Mind of the Market. Compassionate Apes, Competitive Humans and Other Tales from Evolutionary Economics*, Times Books, New York 2008; L. Barrett, R. Dunbar, J. Lycett, *Human Evolutionary Psychology*, Palgrave Macmillan, New York 2002; B.E. Wexler, *Brain and Culture. Neurobiology, Ideology and Social Change*, A Bradford Book MIT Press, London-Cambridge Mass. 2008, pp. 85-137.

369 Cf. R.H. Frank, *The Economic Naturalist. In Search of Explanations for Everyday Enigmas*, Perseus Books, New York 2007, pp. 163-182.

Chapter 13
Evolutionary limitations to human rationality in human resources management

Introduction

Modern social sciences now face challenges related to the development of the natural sciences. The traditional dualistic point of view has so far distinguished the domain of natural sciences and of humanist and social sciences. However, it seems that over the last few decades this traditional division into 'two cultures[370]' has started to break, due to the impressive development of the natural sciences. More and more often, human behaviour and actions are being explained by research fields combining such disciplines as biology, psychology, economics, sociology and information science. Examples of such a cognitively effective hybrid can be seen in the newer disciplines of cognitive science, behavioural economics, neuroscience and evolutionary psychology[371]. The organization theory and management are also facing a challenge related to using the latest results of the natural sciences' research, and confronting them with the established paradigms and theories. An especially interesting field of research is human resources management, based as it is on a broader concept of human behaviour and nature.

The aim of this chapter is to analyse the cognitive consequences of the neoevolutionary paradigm in human resources management, concerning the aspect of decision-making rationality. So far, the results of research in socio-biology, cognitive science, evolutionary psychology and behavioural economics have been, to a large extent, ignored. However, the framework of a new neoevolutionary paradigm of social sciences is being created, which will probably clear up the field of research into human behaviour, and also in relation to organisation and management. Such a deep change of cognitive perspective will also entail significant consequences for human resources management. Thus, it is worth examining the vision of human nature proposed by evolutionism from the point of view of the decision-making rationality in human resources management.

---

370 C.P. Snow, *The Two Cultures.* London: Cambridge University Press, 1959, p. 3.
371 D.M. Buss, *Evolutionary Psychology. The New Science of the Mind,* Pearson, Boston 2008, pp. 36-69.

The evolutionarily limited rationality of human resources processes

When the research of the neoevolutionary current is applied to organisational activities – and also when looking from the economic perspective – it points to significant limitations on decision-making rationality, as a consequence of 'human nature'. People are a 'vehicle of genes', and inherit the mechanism of feedback between the environment and genes. This is aimed at genetic replication, which means that 'human nature' is not infinitely flexible and cannot perfectly correspond to the rules of rational development of an organisation[372]. The most important limitations concern decision-making rationality, which are about interpersonal contact, and are therefore related to most human resources processes. These specific barriers to decision-making rationality concern, for example, treating oneself and one's kin in a preferential way, the intuitive and subconscious importance of the decision-making mechanism, perceptive and interpretative illusions and stereotypes related to treating other people, and cognitive and emotional limitations when making personal decisions.

A biological consequence of the need for genetic replication is protection and treating oneself and one's kin in a preferential way, in comparison to others. This is the source of bias and nepotism, inscribed in human nature, which influences human resources decisions, and not only in family enterprises. This tendency is limited to a certain degree by social norms aimed at limiting nepotism, which can be interpreted as a general mechanism protecting genetic pools excluded by nepotism.

Conscious and rational decision-making mechanisms are only the tip of the iceberg and the youngest part of the human brain, while – as neurobiological research proves – decisions are made on numerous levels of the brain, often in the blink of an eye, based on very limited information[373]. The evolutionary justification for such decisions used to be the stakes related to survival (e.g. immediate decision to flight or fight)[374]. Therefore, human actions often entail only conscious rationalisation of behaviour which is hidden in unconscious layers, called intuition or the subconscious. Human resources decisions are still often related to the sphere of such rationalised behaviour. Persecuting people who pose a threat or are potential rivals, exploiting subordinates of a lower

---

372 R. Dawkins, *The Selfish Gene*, op. cit.

373 M. Gladwell, *Blink. The Power of Thinking Without Thinking*, Time Warner Book Group, New York 2005.

374 Cf. H.C. Barrett, "Adaptations to Predators and Prey" in: *The Handbook of Evolutionary Psychology*, D.M. Buss (ed.), Wiley, New York 2005, pp. 200-223.

group status, choosing and stigmatising a scapegoat, enhancing group identification by finding an enemy, are just a few examples of intuitive social games, hidden in seemingly rational human resources decisions.

The human cognitive system, which has evolved in an environment full of natural dangers, is not a mechanism of fully logical and rational decision-making. An important role in human functioning is played by perceptive and interpretative illusions and stereotypes, which distance the real model of decision-making from the ideal of rationality and logic. Evolutionary psychologists and behavioural economists point to research which explicitly proves that the same tasks are solved far more effectively from the perspective of logic when they are related to social context and interest[375]. This example shows that the human mind has evolved towards finding evolutionary fraudsters, and not solving abstract logical tasks. Stereotypes serve as ready-made cognitive patterns, which are remembered and perceived thanks to an emotional charge. They put in order the general categories and make it very difficult to treat people from highly stigmatised groups in an individual way. In the case of human resources management, commonly known examples of perceptive and interpretative illusions which influence the effectiveness of recruitment, are the First Impression Effect and the Halo Effect[376].

Emotions play the key role in human behaviour, including the decision-making process. Somatic signals warn against choosing variants which are subconsciously interpreted as the most risky, and limit the number of available options in the case of complex and multi-layer decisions[377]. Emotions also play the key role in human resources decisions. Emotional ties between a superior and their subordinates decrease the possibility of imposing sanctions. Decisions against employees often require rationalisation on the part of managers. Unlikely as it may seem, liking or aversion are among the key reasons for keeping or dismissing employees.

Behavioural economics as a discipline concentrates on the limitations on the rationality of economic activities, rooted in the evolutionary human nature[378]. A research programme in the field, carried out from the 1970s until now by A. Tversky, D. Kahneman, C. Camerer, R. Thaler, P. Slavic, T. Gilovich and

375 M.E. Price, L. Cosmides, J. Tooby, "Punitive Sentiment as an Anti-free Rider Psychological Device", *Evolution and Human Behaviour* 2002, vol. 23, no. 3, pp. 203-231.

376 Cf. W.F. Cascio, *Managing Human Resources. Productivity. Quality of Work Life, Profits*. McGraw-Hill, New York 1989, pp. 186-210.

377 A.R. Damasio, *Descartes' Error: Emotion, Reason and the Human Brain*, Putnam, New York 1994.

378 *Advances in Behavioural Economics*, C.F. Camerer, G. Loewenstein, M. Rabin (eds.), Princeton University Press, Princeton NJ 2001.

others, focuses on cognitive illusions and fallacies rooted in human nature[379]. As a result, several universal cognitive illusions rooted in evolution have been described, and it seems that some of these cognitive delusions play an important role in human resources management.

'Representative fallacy' indicates that people – in situations requiring them to make statistical evaluations – use a limited number of heuristics, which results in the lack of adequate assessment of the probability of an event[380]. 'Availability fallacy' consists in assessing probability and making generalisations based only on examples that are easily and immediately available[381]. For example, evaluation of the probability of a plane crash in comparison to other catastrophes would be highly exaggerated due to the overrepresentation of information concerning plane crashes in the mass media[382]. 'Hindsight bias' is the tendency to interpret the past, so that it fits the current state of knowledge. It is a subconscious, selective use of memory and interpretation of past events, so that they are in accordance with present opinions[383]. 'Confirmation bias' means looking only for information confirming initial assumptions and rejecting data which could deny the propagated opinions[384]. The 'endowment effect' shows that the subjective value of an object for its owner is usually much higher than its value as estimated by a potential purchaser[385].

The sources of the illusions presented are rooted in the evolutionary nature of the human cognitive system. The natural adaptation of our species is related to adequate evaluation of small numbers, while probability is an abstract category which people do not comprehend intuitively. Becoming adjusted to life in a small group also stems from generalisations based on available examples. The tendency to confirm opinions is more difficult to interpret, although it

---

379 T. Gilovich, D. Griffin, D. Kahneman, *Heuristics and Biases: The Psychology of Intuitive Judgment*, Cambridge University Press, New York 2002.

380 A. Tversky, D. Kahneman, "Availability: A Heuristics for Judging Frequency and Probability" in: *Judgment Under Uncertainty: Heuristics and Biases*, D. Kahneman, P. Slovic, A. Tversky (eds.), Cambridge University Press, New York 1982.

381 Ibid., p. 163.

382 B. Combs, P. Slovic, "Newspaper Coverage of Causes of Death", *Journalism Quarterly* 1979, no. 56, pp. 837-843.

383 B. Frischhoff, "For Those Condemned to Study Past: Heuristics and Biases in Hindsight" in: *Judgment Under Uncertainty: Heuristics and Biases*, D. Kahneman, P. Slovic, A. Tversky (eds.), Cambridge University Press, New York 1982, pp. 335-350.

384 R. Nickerson, "Confirmation Bias: A Ubiquitous Phenomenon in Many Guises", *Review of General Psychology* 1998, no. 2, pp. 175-220.

385 R. Thaler, D. Kahneman, J. Knetsch, "Experimental Tests of the Endowment Effect and the Coase Theorem", *Journal of Political Economy* 1990, December.

seems that it is based on the mechanism of emotional support for the decision-making effect. Decisions made should be consistently implemented, otherwise they are no longer functional. Another evolutionary source of the 'confirmation bias' may be enhancement of the social group identity and the identification of individuals with the community, the consequence of which is aversion to strangers. 'Endowment effect' and aversion to losses are probably related to the limited material resources used for survival and reproduction in primitive groups. The indicated evolutionary limitations on rationality have a significant influence on human resources management.

Human resources from the Darwinist perspective

An analysis of the consequences of the abovementioned limitations on decision-making rationality in human resources management, on the one hand takes into consideration the results of modern research, mostly related to evolutionary psychology, and on the other proposes their comparison with human resources processes[386]. The abovementioned limitations on decision-making rationality in human resources management have been compared with human resources strategies and processes (human resources recruitment, motivation and development).

Table 8. Human resources strategy and processes vs. evolutionary pressure

Human resources strategy and processes vs. evolutionary pressure	**Human resources strategy**	**Human resources process (recruitment, motivation and development)**
Treating oneself and one's relatives in a preferential way	Strategy secures one's own and relatives' interests	Tendency to nepotism and old-boyism
Intuitive and subconscious decision-making	Evolutionary, emergent, intuitive strategies	Intuitive selection, motivation and development of the human resources, rationalisation of decisions
Stereotypes in the perception of social situations	Ossified patterns of planning, implementing and controlling, and a mechanistic model of human resources management	Deep-rooted stereotypes concerning gender, ethnic, racial or age issues, and stigmatisation

386 Cf. S.M. Colarelli, *No Best Way. An Evolutionary Perspective on Human Resource Management*, Praeger, London 2003.

Cognitive and emotional limitations when making decisions related to human resources	Limited data processing (dustbin model) and the emotive function of human resources strategy	Influence of liking or aversion on managerial decisions concerning human resources

Source: Own work.

1. **Treating oneself and one's relatives in a preferential way.** The willingness to secure, in the first place, the interests of oneself and one's relatives is rooted in human nature. This is why human resources strategy and processes should combine the individual interests of the decision-maker with the development of the organisation. Moreover, organisations (such as family companies) should have mechanisms in place preventing nepotism, or the consequences of nepotism that have gone too far. Construction of an organisational order with an inherent contradiction between the individual interest of the decision-makers and the development of the organisation is a utopian ideal.
2. **Intuitive and subconscious decision-making** concerning strategy and human resources is an inevitable consequence of the construction of human cognitive systems. However, it seems appropriate to formulate rules for making decisions which do not require immediate action based on very limited knowledge, especially at the strategic level. Possible solutions include the participation of other people in decision-making processes, inter-subjective methods of gathering and analysing data, the participation of neutral consultants, and other techniques which decrease the possibilities for making mistakes. Furthermore, it seems that any attempt to eliminate intuition from the process of decision-making is pointless, especially in relation to tactical and operational decisions, but also in relation to subconscious creative processes.
3. **Stereotypes in the perception of social situations**, or the superficial and emotional evaluation of different social groups, have a significant influence on human resources decisions, even if the stereotypes function only on the subconscious level. There has been much research and work concerning the phenomenon of stereotyping and stigmatisation of women and the limiting of their professional promotion ('glass ceiling' and 'sticky floor' syndromes). There are also rich empirical materials related to national and ethnic stereotypes which influence human resources decisions. In some situations, even the process of strategic planning, including human resources strategies in organisations, becomes a stereotype, understood as an ossified cognitive pattern.

4. **Cognitive and emotional limitations when making decisions related to human resources.** Having limited possibilities concerning short-term and long-term memory, people are not able to process large numbers of decision variants. The process of making decisions, including strategic ones, is supported by emotive mechanisms. However, elimination of some of the variants does not consist in calculating profit based on algorithms and data, but in applying heuristics. Therefore, there is a higher probability of error, or even a tendency to repeat certain errors. In the sphere of human resources, we usually face decisions concerning specific people with whom we have different emotional relations. Thus, even those managers who are able to distance themselves from personal issues are always subject to emotional pressure related to human resources decisions.

From the point of view of human resources processes, the consequences of cognitive illusions described by behavioural economics (Table 9) are another important issue.

Table 9. The consequences of chosen cognitive illusions for human resources processes

Illusion	Consequences for human resources processes
Representative fallacy	1. A stereotypical image of employees in relation to recruitment, motivation and development. 2. Creating a narration concerning employees in case of the lack of information.
Availability fallacy	1. Projection of familiar behaviour patterns onto the actions of new employees. 2. Limiting the creativity and innovativeness of employees by enhancing familiar behaviour patterns
Hindsight bias	1. Rationalisation of own and employees actions, distorting reality. 2. *Post factum* justifications of strategy and planning.
Confirmation bias	1. Selecting market research and information in order to justify human resources decisions made. 2. Rejecting information that questions the decisions made. 3. Limiting decision variants to extreme options (e.g. dismissing or keeping an employee). 4. Positive interpretation of one's own actions, negative interpretation of the actions of others.
Endowment effect	1. Resisting changes in human resources decisions. 2. Decreasing the tendency to risk. 3. Overestimating human resources.

Source: Own work.

Perceptive and interpretative illusions limit the choice of decision variants and the analysis of information in human resources processes. These are the result of economisation and integration of perception processes, which are of a selective character. Human resources strategies are often chosen on an ad hoc basis and depend on the needs, perception and interest of the decision-makers. This is accompanied by rationalisation indicating that the decisions were made based on the results of data analysis. Similarly to human resources processes, decisions concerning employment, dismissal and rewards are based on a superficial perception and interpretation of the decision-maker, who is often influenced by illusions.

Summary

The limitations on decision-making rationality related to human resources described in this chapter take the form of tendencies often found in organisations, although they are not bound to be present there. There is no simple correlation between the levels of genes, individuals, social groups and organisations. Each of the levels is of an emergent character and adds its own system rules to the level below. Thus, we are not condemned to eternal nepotism and organisational illusions in the human resources area, although we do tend to be influenced by them.

In light of the research carried out in the fields of evolutionary psychology, behavioural economics, cognitive science, neuroscience and sociology, one could note that the rationality of human actions is limited, not only by access to market information, but also by the evolutionary character of the human cognitive system, which is functionally adjusted to social activities in a primitive group and not complex mass societies and bureaucratic organisations. Naturally, the examples presented of limitations on the rationality of human resources decisions which have evolutionary sources do not exhaust the whole range of variables interfering in the human resources function. However, they do clearly show that from the perspective of human resources management, the vision of *Homo economicus* is as important as *Homo biologicus* and *Homo sociologicus*[387] – M. Shermer even proposes the term *Homo evonomicus*[388]. Finally, the over-rationalised vision of human nature is not confirmed by the

387 C. Elworthy, *Homo Biologicus. An Evolutionary Model for the Human Sciences*, Duncker & Humblot, Berlin 1993 (Internet).

388 M. Shermer, *The Mind of the Market. Compassionate Apes, Competitive Humans and Other Tales from Evolutionary Economics*, Times Books, New York 2008, pp. 188-190.

basic research carried out by neoevolutionism. From the point of view of human resources management, this means it is necessary to take into consideration intuition, the subconscious and emotions on the level of strategy and human resources processes.

Conclusions

Applying the neoevolutionary perspective to social sciences leads to creative results. It allows for a verified theory describing human activities, appropriate for use in a number of social sciences. Modern evolutionary psychology is more and more effective in explaining and foreseeing human behaviour, often distancing itself from a purely behaviourist vision of human nature. Neuroscience and cognitive science describe and model human behaviour on the level of brain functioning. Primatology points to the roots of human social and cognitive skills based on research into other primates. Anthropology, making use of the palaeo-anthropological research, also offers an increasingly precise description of how primitive communities and human cultures formed. Behavioural economics has been conducting experimental studies on the human decision-making process, which has lead to results that fit coherently with the neoevolutionary paradigm. Therefore, it seems vital that the management sciences take up the challenge too.

Neoevolutionism is the subject of many controversies, related mostly to its departure from the traditional vision of people and society rooted in European culture. Neoevolutionism is reductionist and undermines the vision of human nature based on subjective and rational decision-making. Its explanations of behaviour refer to deep motivations hidden in the human mind, which are related to the evolutionary past. For example, family ties are a result of 'gene selfishness', the striving for power and rivalry are mechanisms of sexual selection, while gender differences can be explained by biological differences in sexual strategies[389]. The question of free will, subjectivity and inter-determinism in decision-making is problematic. At the same time, neoevolutionism provides us with credible knowledge about the biological basis for the spheres which define the essence of humanity, such as morality, interpersonal ties, and language and culture, although it does not allow for description of the process of their emergence in human societies. The fact is, *Homo sapiens* differ from other primates, but research shows that the differences only concern the concentration of features or skills, which still do not explain qualitative changes in behaviour.

Thus, this book presents a fairly anthropocentric point of view, treating the achievements of mankind as the highest level of the development of biological cognitive complexity. R. Dawkins noticed that anthropocentrism is an illusion, as each species adjusts itself to its niche. In this sense then, people, just like

389 D.M. Buss, *Evolutionary Psychology. The New Science of the Mind*, Pearson, Boston 2008.

other species, are neither 'superior' nor 'ultimate' beings[390]. Both in terms of their reach and the effectiveness of reproduction, the true 'masters' of the Earth are bacteria, not humans[391].

However, recognising the cognitive effectiveness of 'Neo-Darwinism', I believe that neoevolutionism, which successfully explains the basis for the symbolic and abstract world of people, is not able to fully describe the identity of mankind. Thus, there is no point in rejecting the works of social sciences *en bloc*, which interpret the human world as an emergent, higher sphere built upon the biological foundations. The world of culture, ethics, and perhaps information as such, has its specific rules, probably rooted in biology and evolution, but they do require examining. The attempts to explain these areas, though going far back, have not yet resulted in any great synthesis or a dominant paradigm. I also place certain hope in memetics as a hypothesis explaining how culture functions. At the current stage of development of the social sciences, I would postulate epistemological and methodological pluralism.

Neoevolutionism can be treated as a valuable proposal for yet another paradigm of the social sciences, which can be confronted with other cognitive perspectives. In the field of research methodology it is possible, or even recommended, to combine methods drawn from different paradigms of social sciences if it might lead to better cognitive effects. Assuming epistemological pluralism leaves open the question of the integration of the research results and theory of social sciences, developed based on different paradigms. In modern times, the key problem is the disproportion between the research results, which however could be overcome in the future. Neoevolutionism is a scientific current in the social sciences, which means it uses scientific methodological patterns. However, it seems possible that an attempt could be made to make a synthesis of the neoevolutionary approach and valuable theories drawn from other paradigms of social sciences.

This book presents the application of evolutionary issues to the social sciences, and especially to the analysis of issues related to the management sciences. The presented framework of paradigm, methodology and research issues, leads to a proposal to distinguish a new research field called 'evolutionary management'. The issues of evolutionary management would be by definition interdisciplinary; a combination of organising and management with evolutionary psychology and behavioural economics. The paradigm of evolutionary management would be coherent with the neoevolutionary

390 R. Dawkins, *Ancestors Tale: A Pilgrimage to the Dawn of Life*, Houghton Mifflin, New York 2004.

391 B. Bryson, *A Short History of Nearly Everything*, Broadway Books, 2003.

conception of the description of human behaviour. This requires assumption of numerous postulates related to basing the management sciences on the basic evolutionary theories of human behaviour.

- Human behaviour is based on the vision of human nature described by neoevolutionism, which means that the processes of organising and management should also be considered from the evolutionary perspective. Organising and management are rooted in the evolutionary, universal rules which govern the functioning of human communities.
- The basic needs and motives for human activities develop in accordance with the evolutionary basis, and include the gene perspective and sexual and natural selection, therefore organisational behaviour is also natural.
- Culture is a mechanism that re-shapes behaviour in relation to evolution, which means it usually develops on a biological basis. An example of this are the social processes that are key to the perspective of management: stratification of power and hierarchy, emergence of leadership, interpersonal communication, individual and group learning.
- Valuable research into individual and group behaviour, which is in accordance with the epistemology of scientific realism and objectivism, should be based on controlled methods, assuring the repeatability of the results, and modelled on the natural sciences. The advantages of this methodology are verificationism and experimental methods including mathematical modelling.

Neoevolutionism seems to be an interesting cognitive perspective for the management and organizational theory, introducing a creative aspect into the theoretical and empirical sphere, related mainly to drawing from other scientific disciplines in the field of theory and the methodology of research. This monograph includes a number of proposals on how to apply neoevolutionary thinking to management. Human resources management is concerned with such issues as motivation, leadership and people management, which are based on theories related to human nature and the nature of a social group. The interpretation of modern research results of evolutionary psychology and behavioural economics will allow development of new effective theories of motivation and leadership. So far, organisational behaviour, understood as a discipline applying the research results of other social sciences to management, has not been concerned with the neoevolutionary approach. Strategic management concerns other factors which influence the making of strategic managerial decisions, which can be rooted in evolutionary models –

organisational culture, for example, may be interpreted as an implementation of the group ties formed in the course of evolution.

The possibility of using the research results and methods of many other disciplines related to the neoevolutionary paradigm may also be important to the management sciences. Valuable results are a consequence of using controlled methods, such as social experiments and observations, which are rarely used in management. The results of research carried out by neuroscience, cognitive science, primatology and paleo-anthropology may be creatively used by the management sciences, both from the point of view of theory and practice. So far, the most interesting results in this field have been provided by behavioural economics and finances, however, they identify themselves to a larger degree with economics than management.

In summary, the neoevolutionary paradigm and the research field it is related to form a new, creative proposal for the development of theory, methodology and practice of management. It is important to find scientists focusing on this research field who can translate the epistemological postulate into valuable research results. Furthermore, it seems pointless to develop a hermetic orthodoxy in the form of social Neo-Darwinism, which rejects the previous output of social sciences. A more sensible solution is an epistemological and methodological pluralism allowing for the integration of different paradigms and research methods.

New Horizons in Management Sciences

Edited by Lukasz Sulkowski

Vol. 1 Lukasz Sulkowski: Neodarwinism in Organization and Management. 2012.

www.peterlang.de

www.ingramcontent.com/pod-product-compliance
Ingram Content Group UK Ltd.
Pitfield, Milton Keynes, MK11 3LW, UK
UKHW021833100926
8556IPUK00004B/310

9 783631 637500